This book belongs to

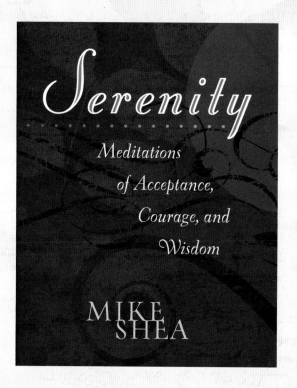

Serenity

Meditations
of Acceptance,
Courage, and
Wisdom

MIKE
SHEA

BroadStreet
PUBLISHING

BroadStreet Publishing Group LLC
Racine, Wisconsin, USA
Broadstreetpublishing.com

Serenity: Meditations of Acceptance, Courage, and Wisdom
© 2015 by Mike Shea

ISBN 978-1-4245-5054-8 (hardcover)
ISBN 978-1-4245-5055-5 (e-book)

Scripture quotations marked (NLT) are taken from the *Holy Bible,*
New Living Translation, copyright © 1996, 2004, 2007. Used by
permission of Tyndale House Publishers, Inc., Carol Stream, Illinois
60188. All rights reserved.

Design by Chris Garborg | www.garborgdesign.com
Editorial services by Michelle Winger | www.literallyprecise.com

Printed in China.

15 16 17 18 19 20 21   7 6 5 4 3 2 1

He has rescued us from the
kingdom of darkness and transferred
us into the Kingdom of his dear
Son, who purchased our freedom
and forgave our sins.

COLOSSIANS 1:13-14 NLT

Dedication

This book is dedicated to my beloved wife,

Peggy, who participated, persevered, and

loved me during each step of the five-month

pilgrimage of writing. Your strength and

words of life were crucial and much needed.

Thank you.

ACKNOWLEDGMENTS

I want to acknowledge the critical roles of those around me whose encouragement allowed this work to be completed. From Serenity Village leadership: Pastor Jeff Hill and wife Monica, Jackson, Doug, Jack, and Mike; from the team at Waters of Life Recovery Ministry: Bishop Earl Gilchrist and wife Pam; from my Tuesday and Wednesday night groups: Pastor Joni, David, and Norm; the many, mighty warriors at Serenity Village whose hugs kept life in perspective; and those whose names are too numerous to mention.

Thank you, Carlton, Michelle, and BroadStreet team for publishing and editing. Your care, respect, and dedication to your strong ministry is so appreciated.

Also on behalf of those who fought the good fight to the best of their ability, and died much too young: God bless your memory. We will keep your legacy alive.

Introduction

This book is birthed from my personal on-going journey of recovery and the many years of being part of a faith-based recovery ministry. It's a pilgrimage to remember that words of death spoken over me in the past can now be exchanged for the Holy Spirit's whispers of life. This isn't about clean time; this is about free time.

God wants to take you to a place where hopelessness is replaced by hope, death is traded for life, words spoken from hurt and emotion become words spoken from respect and wisdom, darkness is exchanged for God's light, depression is substituted for action and service, and addiction is swapped for recovery.

These devotionals are your story and mine—an imperfect journey, by imperfect ruffians into the loving arms of the Father. We are saved by the blood of Jesus, and encouraged by the Holy Spirit to continue the recovery journey his way, not ours. Recovery is possible.

What I've witnessed during ten years of observing over one thousand addicts come through the doors of Serenity Village is recorded on these pages. Recovery is about being taught by a servant of God to be a servant of God, and embracing practical, Biblical principles. It's essential to be as desperate for your recovery as you were for your addiction.

Recovery happens when you admit you're absolutely poor in spirit. You submit to God first, in all things—he comes before family, jobs, relationships...everything. To seek God's will for you and to be accountable with someone else are both critical components.

Jesus says love is the greatest commandment, and his love is expressed through you to others. Actions speak louder than words. God desires to activate you into his service, help break generational curses, and love other addicts into recovery.

God, I humbly ask you to speak through your words. I request your living Word will penetrate deeply. Soften hearts and open eyes. I pray the words in this book will be a blessing to those struggling, and an encouragement for those walking on your path. Help them all to recover and live in freedom. In Jesus' name. Amen.

Climb into Jesus' lap now to rest, simply because you can.

MIKE SHEA

TABLE OF CONTENTS

A Resolution

The start of a new year is a great time to check on your recovery. The statistics show that 90% of resolutions fail within thirty days. Strong starters are weak finishers, and best intentions are left in tatters. God saved you because of his mercy, and he renews you by the Holy Spirit. For this very reason, make every effort to add to your faith goodness, knowledge, self-control, perseverance, godliness, mutual affection, and love.

The true measure of your faith walk is whether or not people even know you're in recovery. Work the Word and it will work you. Study God's Word so you can activate the Word in daily life.

God's people spent forty years wandering because of their complaining. How is your level of gratitude? Who are you listening to—God, the flesh, or the lies of the enemy? Stand firm in your faith and resist the devil during times of suffering. To skip a meeting or miss a mentor call are little compromises that begin to seep into your recovery and can eventually take you out.

Lord, I need your help to examine myself, rather than others. I pray I will remember what you brought me out of and how bad it was. Thank you for the light and joy that are now mine. Amen.

TITUS 3:5; 2 PETER 1:5-9; 2 TIMOTHY 2:15; GALATIANS 5:9

What Do You Allow In?

God knows your very next thought. He put in you everything you need to seek and serve him—beginning with knowing when he's nudging you. A ship doesn't sink when it's in the water; it sinks when the water gets in. You can be in chaos, but you'll only go down when the chaos gets in you. God uses all your experiences to reveal himself to you. God's ready to help, so don't be afraid. That which you allow in can affect your day.

The chaos of the past wants to get in. Weariness and burdens that you allow in can sink your recovery ship. God's purpose for you is to be fruitful and productive in the place he sets you. This season he has purposed for you a window of opportunity to recover.

Today, discover the priceless value God places upon you. Connect with the radical, excessive love the Father has for you. Nothing in all creation will be able to separate you from the love of the Father that's in his Son.

Lord, thanks for this appointed time to discover my purpose. I pray for strength to keep chaos from sinking my recovery ship. I pray for revelation, not information. Amen.

Hebrews 13:6; Romans 8:1, 39; Ecclesiastes 3:1

The Devil's Snare

The Hebrew word for offense is *skandalone*—where the bait is attached in the trap. Offense will come: the enemy sets the bait to attract, and the snare to catch you. *Oh, I don't get offended, or offend anyone. Really!* Offense is sin: hurting others, causing resentment and anger. Be watchful for the devil's snare.

In relationships, unmet expectations can cause you to be offended. You're limited to only receive what you perceive someone to be. If you have trust issues, it's difficult to receive. When looking for others to fulfill your needs, relationships self-destruct.

When you are offended, you operate in what you believe to be true. It should be this, or it could be that. This isn't God's way, and he will not adjust the truth to what you believe. The Bible says those who are not offended are blessed.

Lord, I desire forgiveness for the many times I have offended you and others. I pray for strength not to cause offense and not to be offended. Amen.

ROMANS 11:9; LUKE 17:1; MATTHEW 11:6

Your Response Defines You

Joseph's brothers sold him into slavery because he was favored by their father. You've experienced favoritism in some way—a prideful attitude, bragging, friction with siblings, betrayal or abandonment by family, or enduring time in prison—with or without walls. Joseph, by his example, provided some good life lessons: He didn't spend a lot of time being a victim and asking why; his focus was on doing the next right thing. When he faced a setback, he didn't take a shortcut. He wasn't defined by his situation but by his response.

When you look too far ahead, the foreboding walls seem impassable. It's only when you start walking in faith and getting closer to those walls of impossibilities that you discover a small door. You would never have seen the door without starting out and getting closer.

When you trust in the Lord, and know he is the rock eternal on which to stand, you start walking by faith. Joseph accepted his assignment from God. Do you dare start walking in faith toward your assignment and accept it regardless of consequences?

Lord, thanks for using all the things I've experienced, even betrayal by those closest, for my good. I'm grateful you love me enough to get me where you desire me to be. Amen.

Genesis 37:5; Isaiah 26:4; Romans 8:28

Bread of Life

Jesus says he is the bread of life. The crowd's many questions were answered when Jesus pointed out their motivation for being with him—he *fed* them. Jesus came to satisfy spiritual hunger, and he invites your participation in the glorious endeavor to set aside physical wants to focus on your spiritual needs. He offered the bread of his flesh that allows us to live forever. Even if you didn't know him at the time, it was his power that lifted you from the darkness of addiction.

It's the Spirit who gives eternal life. All your efforts and willpower accomplish nothing. You're not capable of coming to Christ—it's a gift from the Father.

When asked if the disciples wanted to leave Jesus, Peter answered, "To whom would we go?" This question is worthy of your response as well. Where would you go? Back to detox, treatment centers, hospitals, jails, prisons, and worse! You need food and light to live: the food is Jesus offering himself on the cross, and the light is his living Word, which illuminates your path.

Father, I pray I will truly receive the gift of your Son.
I love your bread of life. Amen.

JOHN 6:26-68; PSALM 119:105

Free to Have a Good Day

When you are faithless, God remains faithful. He was faithful even during your many times of doubt and unbelief. In the darkest days of addiction, fueled by depression, pain, and manic-bipolar episodes, God was faithful. While suffering from guilt and shame so intense that suicide seemed the only path to peace, God was faithful. Whether in detox, a psych ward, treatment, on the streets, or in prison, God was faithful. The creator has a plan and purpose for you, and his faithfulness gave you just enough hope to beat back the dense fog of darkness enveloping you.

God's faithfulness to you is evident in that you're still breathing. He gifted you the miracle of another chance to recover. Be strong in the grace that is in Christ Jesus. God lifted you when your weakened legs couldn't stand, he holds you while you walk your steps of recovery, and he empowers you to have a good day in spite of bad things happening.

You can choose what kind of day you'll have, but the faithfulness of God says you're free to have a good day, every day. Expect your day to go well.

Lord, thanks for being faithful, even when my faith was miserably non-existent. I pray for the courage to expect a good day. Amen.

2 TIMOTHY 2:1, 13; EPHESIANS 6:13

All God Has for You

The chaos of the past has trained you to pray emergency room prayers and expect fast food answers. What you think is good might not be good for you, and your timing and God's timing will always be at odds.

In recovery, you're learning to pray about everything and not worry about anything. It's okay to tell God what you need, and to thank him for all he's done, but it's time to exchange your perceived wants for actual needs. Trust that God is working on your situation even when nothing seems to be happening. He doesn't need your help!

You no longer have to ask God for less than what he has for you. Instead of praying for your situation to change, give it to God to work out what's best. After prayer, it's okay to wonder if God heard you. God knows the proper time and season to release his answers to your prayers. In truth, God's also working on getting you to the place where you can receive with power and be made new.

Lord, I praise you for the many prayers answered. I thank you for releasing grace even when I'm not asking for it. Amen.

PHILIPPIANS 4:6-7; JAMES 4:2-3; ROMANS 10:17

An Active Faith Walk

Trust that your help comes from the creator. God gives you the assurance and hope that he's watching over your recovery and protecting you whenever the enemy suggests that you've failed in the past and you will fail again. The all-powerful, majestic God is your shade. He keeps you from harm and he watches your every move. He invites you to participate in an active faith walk where you are responsible for your effort and you let him be in charge of the outcome.

Your flesh can take a wrong turn out of the church parking lot. Because you're still capable of mass destruction, you need God on a minute-to-minute basis.

In a reckless display of complete abandon, give God your recovery. He will strengthen, help, and uphold you with his victorious right hand. Fight for your recovery. Rest in him when you feel overwhelmed. God's presence is the only place on this earth to find rest and be refreshed.

Lord, I pray for strength to fight for my recovery. I need your constant grace because I am poor in spirit. Amen.

PSALMS 5-8,121:1-2; ISAIAH 41:10

You'll Get through This

The false facade of thinking more highly of yourself than of others has to go; it's a mask everyone has worn. A subtle smokescreen from the pit of hell declares that what you did in the past disqualifies you from the Father's unconditional love. When you feel worthless, you tell others they're unworthy; when you feel judged, you'll judge others; and when you feel guilty, you'll pronounce others guilty. You no longer have to pretend to be someone you're not.

In recovery, it's critical to accept the truth that your old life is gone. Christ's new life for you has begun. A fresh start for a new day, a new you. God reconciled the world to himself, making all things new. Jesus' love compels you to places never imagined or dreamed of.

Jesus died so you no longer live for yourself, but for him. As you leave the "old man" the enemy declares you to be, and embrace the "new man" God says you are, there will be opposition. That's okay. You'll get through this—just don't quit.

Lord, I pray I will treat others better, thinking less of myself. I pray for grace for the times my false mask sneaks back onto my face. Amen.

2 CORINTHIANS 5:15-17; GALATIANS 5:14-17

Confession Is Critical

In recovery, it's critical to confess your human frailties, imperfections, and shortcomings to God and others. God will forgive you and wash you clean. It's not easy to admit your deepest secrets because of the fear that others won't accept you. You need to release the truth in order to remove what hinders you from moving forward. Pride, and the enemy's lie that no one needs to know, comes against the need to share. Release your stuff to receive God's stuff.

God is dependable. He has factored into your recovery the road to forgiveness. His beloved Son died to pardon your transgressions, and his faithfulness is the starting point for your act of faith to confess. When you confess your sins and pray with others you become healed and whole. This is essential to your recovery.

As you trust your new, intimate relationship with the Son of God, trusting others becomes easier.

Lord, I pray I will share what I want to keep inside. I pray for trust to reveal to others that which is holding me back. Amen.

1 JOHN 1:9; JAMES 5:16; PSALM 51:7

Lift Another Higher

God's love flows to you in spite of your past. It was waiting with open arms the moment you reached total brokenness. Recovery began the instant you admitted you were powerless. Everyone on the planet is recovering from something. A mustard seed of willingness is all that's needed to take a baby step out of addiction and into God's unique witness protection program. When the Lord delights in your journey, he makes your steps firm. Even if you stumble, you won't fall; he's got you. It's your season to recover.

Nothing, absolutely nothing, brings you into recovery except God. It's critical to remember the torture and despair you experienced during your addiction. God used your shame and pain to lift you out of the slimy pit and set your feet on a rock. He gave you a firm place to stand. He takes the most unlovable and unworthy people on the planet and promotes them into recovery.

Use your time wisely to learn and practice the godly principle of serving others. The miracle is when selfish and ungrateful people lift other unlovable people above themselves.

Lord, I pray I will lift others above myself like you did for me. I pray I will learn and practice your principle of serving others in recovery. Amen.

PSALMS 37:23-24, 40:2

Live By Believing

You cannot be in creation without getting in touch with the creator. As you diligently search for God, he reveals his presence in the tiniest details of your life in the most extraordinary ways. During moments of weariness, when your strength is not sufficient, his strength is. When life's struggles are about to take you out, his grace and power are made perfect in your weakness. Acceptance of his power begins with trust. This is challenging because past broken promises, improper sexual advances, harassment, or verbal attacks can violate our trust in others.

The attempts by the enemy to assassinate the person God created you to be have pressed you on every side; yet you're not crushed. You're still standing. You're perplexed, but don't give up and quit. To become free from past transgressions, ask the Father to reveal himself. His grace and power will give you the courage and strength to forgive others.

God will give you all you need one day at a time. Chaos is exchanged for orderliness, doubt and fear diminish, violators of your trust are forgiven, and healing of injuries begins.

Lord, I pray I will know recovery is an inside job, not an outside one. I pray to live by believing, not by seeing, through the eyes of the Holy Spirit. Amen.

2 CORINTHIANS 4:8, 5:5-7, 12:9; MATTHEW 6:32-33

God Has Called You

Your flesh comes against your recovery with spiritual warfare you never knew existed. It's been going on since your birth. The enemy keeps throwing toxic darts of confusion, chaos, condemnation, and shame to get you to climb back onto his extreme specialized torture rack. That's okay. Opposition means you're on the right track. You've searched and googled everything to figure out a plan to get you where you desired to be, to no avail. In recovery, you're now in the perfect place to see what God has for you.

God desires for you to receive his revelation of the promises and assignment he placed in you at birth. You haven't disqualified yourself, but it's up to you to walk into what he's always had for you. God works for the good of those who love him, who have been called according to his purpose.

It's extremely critical for you to know God chose you, called you, justifies you, and glorifies you. You've been given abundant grace and mercy for your healing in order to comfort those in trouble with the comfort you received from God. Will it be his purpose, or your purpose?

Lord, I pray with thanksgiving for the new song you put into my once hardened heart. I pray for grace to give up, and give in—to you. Amen.

ROMANS 8:28-30; 2 CORINTHIANS 1:3-4; PSALM 40:3

Light in the Lord

As you trust God more, your excuses and reasons for continuing to embrace your false self-diminish. As one of his adopted kids, live a life of love, just as Christ loved you and gave himself up for you as a fragrant offering and sacrifice to God. He didn't do this to get anything *from* you, he did it to give everything *to* you. You're the beloved of Jesus, and you are worthy to receive the love of the Father as you are, not as you should be. He meets you where you are.

This is a process. You've probably beat yourself up for years when falling short, and believed yourself unworthy of any good thing. Once you were in darkness, but now you're in the light. It's refreshing to be out of the murkiness and fog to operate in the Son-light where clarity and truth reveal the path of recovery ahead. Dare to take your eyes off yourself, grab onto Jesus' hand, and walk with him through your day.

It's extremely critical to check with your mentor on how your day looks to them. They will help keep your light shining.

Lord, I pray to live as one of your adopted kids—in freedom. I pray for willingness to call my mentor when I am struggling. Amen.

EPHESIANS 5:2, 8

God Works Out the Details

In your humanness, you can easily get ensnared when wondering about your present suffering. You ran from troubles in the past, isolated when things seemed overwhelming, and medicated the pain. The blessing now is you have the choice to face the fear and not run. Let go, and let God deal with it.

With God, there can't be any comparison to your present difficulties and the glory which will be revealed in and through you. Yes, there will be times when you're caught between God's perfect timing and yours. That's okay. Trust that God is who he says he is, and that he will do what he says. This comes against the enemy's counterfeit gospel of busyness and instant gratification.

There will be times of conforming to values which are not God's, when people-pleasing becomes your daily devotion, when earning your way to heaven replaces grace, and when impatience with God's timing arises. At times, you may wonder if Jesus' shed blood covers the multitude of your sins. Ease up on yourself and rejoice; the Holy Spirit helps in your weakness and gives you the strength to stay and recover.

Lord, I pray for courage to ask, seek, and knock on your door. I pray for grace to receive, find, and walk through your open door. Amen.

ROMANS 8:18, 26-28; MATTHEW 7:7-8

Let God Choose

The times you declare with some degree of self-flattery, "I chose God," falls short. You didn't choose him. He chose you and put you into the world to bear fruit. Do we seriously believe that we had the power to choose him when broken by sarcasm and insults, flat on our faces, reduced to nothing, without a shoulder to cry on? God chose to lift us from the darkness to reveal his eternal, unconditional love at the very moment we were the least deserving and most undesirable people on the planet.

Your opportunity to recover from addiction came from Jesus' choice to leave his heavenly throne to live, love, and die for you. He chose to do the will of his Father. His shed blood washed your slate clean of all sin and rescued you from the lifestyle you chose to embrace. Without Jesus' choice, you would have none!

The bottom line is that the God of creation, the Lord and Savior, shows mercy and compassion to anyone he chooses... and he chose *you*! Your best choice today is to allow God to choose your path through any circumstance you're facing.

Lord, I pray to choose to walk your path today. Thanks for showing mercy and compassion in choosing me. Amen.

JOHN 15:16; PSALM 69:20; ROMANS 9:15-16; JOSHUA 24:15

Just Around the Corner

Jesus—by taking your past and future sins upon himself—unconditionally pardoned you by his tender mercy. Your addiction took you much farther than you ever could have imagined. God demonstrated his love when you were powerless and lost in sin. He justified you and brought you into his camp to no longer experience separation from him. St. Patrick, in a dynamic prayer, spoke of God's presence surrounding us from head to toe and around every square inch of our physical bodies from the day we were born.

As you rest in the Father's lap, the same longing he has for you is transferred into your very being. You get in touch with his longing for another soul in distress and it gives you purpose. Allow God to love another unlovable through you, as he first loved you.

When you love others, you experience opposition. Don't be surprised at the fiery trials that test you. The pressure brought against you during your daily walk in faith-based recovery is the barometer that measures if you're on the right track. God needs you for kingdom business.

Lord, I'm grateful trials allow me to participate in what you experienced. I'm thankful your glory is just around the corner. Amen.

ROMANS 5:6-8; 1 PETER 4:12-13

Love that Saves and Protects

The eyes of your heart become focused to fully grasp the hope God has called you to and the riches of his inheritance. His incomparably great power is given to those who believe. These are the most radical, intense, unconventional words spoken in Scriptures to digest, receive, and believe. Your flesh and soul have no capacity to accept the contract written in Jesus' blood. By faith, the same power which raised Jesus from the dead is now in you.

The Father in heaven calls you to belong to him. You're more than a conqueror through him. The battle in your mind is unbearable at times because the war you're in is the war against yourself. In his power, you can die to self and take captive both the enemy's lies and the stubbornness of the flesh.

Death, life, angels, and demons can't separate you from God's love. Fear of today and worry about tomorrow, or even the powers of hell, can't keep God's love away. The Father's love saves and protects you.

Lord, I pray to go deeper into your love which saves and protects. I pray to trust your awesome power to do kingdom business. Amen.

Ephesians 1:18-19; Romans 8:37-39

Listen Carefully

When you seek God with a humble heart and listen very carefully to the truth of his Word, you'll not drift away. To be silent and still and hear his whisper is not an easy task. You can even get distracted during prayer and devotions. In the flesh, you're your own worst enemy. It's essential to identify that your corrupt nature is opposed to your spiritual nature. It is hostile to God, and it has a limited perspective and view.

It's critical for your recovery and new life in freedom to cherish the moments you rest in Jesus' lap and hear the heartbeat of the Son of God. He loves you unconditionally in the most radical way. He nurtures and feeds your spirit, and arms you with wisdom to guide you on the peaceful path to life.

Wisdom is practical discernment with clarity. It helps you make sound and wise choices in the midst of the difficult circumstances of the day. God encourages you to ask for wisdom, and he will gladly give it to you.

Lord, I praise you for being so patient with me. I pray for courage to ask for wisdom when my flesh is screaming to be in control. Amen.

HEBREWS 2:1; ROMANS 8:7; GALATIANS 5:17; PROVERBS 3:18; JAMES 1:5

Asking for Help

If you choose not to work on your recovery, you're choosing to get high! The little foxes will creep in and erode your recovery foundation. When you don't choose God's truth, you're inadvertently choosing the devil's lie. It's critical to understand that no choice is making a choice. It's extremely dangerous when you choose to entertain doubt, fear, anger, low self-esteem, condemnation, worry, anxiety, and lies. God's given you the authority to use his weapons to knock down the strongholds of human reasoning and to destroy false arguments.

This is about progress, a day at a time, to let go and let God. You're no longer a slave but God's own child, and everything he has belongs to you. The Father gives you authority to move out of your mind and stop being critical of yourself for the times you fall short. You actually glorify God by asking for his help, submitting to his authority, and knowing Jesus' blood already covers the circumstance you're so worried about.

Just as you believed who the enemy said you were, it's okay to now receive who God says you are—one of his kids.

Lord, I pray I will forget yesterday and receive what you've got for me today. I desire to throw a grateful party for you rather than a hissy-fit for me.

JOHN 8:32; 2 CORINTHIANS 10:3-4; GALATIANS 4:7

The Power Is in His Strength

Do you associate power with what you can do, or what God can do for you? Today's battles can't be fought with yesterday's strength. It's insanity to keep doing what's never worked and believe the result will be different this time. You're learning, in recovery, that the only victory you'll experience is doing things God's way. It's time to take the wind out of the sails of self-pity, confront your pride, and stop blaming others for your wrong choices. Give God a shot; you've tried everything else!

Whatever hard times you're going through, they have no comparison to the coming good times. Endure, persevere, and don't give up! Don't listen to other's sarcasm, criticism, judgment, or condemnation. Those are attacks against your peace in Christ.

Remember, the only time a weapon can prosper against you is when you choose to entertain it. Human reasoning will never get you to God; it is always a dead-end. The Spirit gives life; the flesh counts for nothing.

Lord, I pray I will quit arguing with myself on what to do, and give it to you. I pray to be on guard so a weapon formed against me won't take me out. Amen.

ROMANS 8:18; ISAIAH 54:17; JOHN 6:63

Stay Hungry

The incessant intellectual thoughts and reasoning rolling through your mind dulls the spiritual hunger for God. The gospel message is not based on human reasoning but on God. It's in your mind that rejection flourishes—you feel denied of all that you thought you should have. It's key to remember the day God picked you out of the miry clay into his loving arms that hold you up forever. He's the place of safety you've been searching for. The Father declares your steps have been orchestrated; there are no wasted steps, no lost opportunities, and there's a purpose for all you've been through.

Trust Abba Father to take you through the raging storms of life—the violence of hurricane winds and intense thunderstorms. He delivers you from the dark night to witness the joy of the bright, morning light—Jesus! Your trust in him grows as you persevere through life's challenges.

God's path for recovery is the gleam of dawn, shining brighter and brighter. You can't have blessing without suffering, triumph without endurance, or victory without a battle. Just don't give up!

Lord, thanks for working on my desire to be obedient, and giving me the power to do what pleases you. I pray I will stick, stay, and remain hungry for you. Amen.

GALATIANS 1:11; DEUTERONOMY 33:27; PROVERBS 4:18;
PHILIPPIANS 2:13

The Fork in the Road

Practically everything the world wants has nothing to do with the design of the creator. When you tip-toe through the world's tulips, the love of what it offers can squeeze out your love for the Father. In a flash, you can choose insanity over God's wisdom and peace. The power of you versus the power of God makes absolutely no sense, yet your pride and ego demand their victory dance of control and manipulation at a huge cost.

Jesus listens to your prayer and empowers you to walk his path to freedom. In a split second, the atmosphere can change and off you go in your Pharisee robes. As you approach the fork in the road, God's Spirit nudges you in the direction most beneficial, yet your stubborn flesh hates to be told what to do. It elbows its way around the Spirit to lead you down the road of falling rocks and another dead-end.

Resist the enemy and the flesh in the name of Jesus, and choose God's smooth, peaceful road. Know there's still a war going on. Arm up!

Lord, I pray the Holy Spirit would be active and breathing in me. I pray for forgiveness for the many times I choose the world over you. Amen.

1 JOHN 2:15-17; ROMANS 8:7

Take It Captive

It's critical to know you're at war. War veterans understand the principle of proper reconnaissance to seek information about enemy positions. You cannot build adequate defense of your perimeter without it; it's a set up to be overrun. The weapons you use aren't the weapons of the world. On the contrary, you have the divine power to demolish strongholds. You've been using weapons that don't work. Only God's superior firepower can blast the enemy's strongholds in your life.

The Father's divine power demolishes arguments and every pretension that sets itself up against you and the knowledge of God. It's your stubborn human nature to listen to deceit and lies before listening to the truth. Aren't you getting tired of arguing with yourself? You can't control what comes into your head, but you're in charge of how long you entertain it.

Deal with arguments and deceit intentionally—release them to God, or rehearse them over and over. Avoid being captured by the enemy again; the torture chamber is worse than before.

Lord, I pray for courage to take captive every thought to make it obedient to you. I pray to be more intentional and strategic with using your weapons because I'm tired of being held captive. Amen.

2 CORINTHIANS 10:3-5

Embrace the Work

You can choose the flesh—slavery and death—or the Spirit—freedom and life. You've made the decision for life many times, yet when adversity strikes, you're medicating your pain and shame in an instant. This is strong stuff that even the apostle Paul dealt with. He pointed out that when we want to do good, we don't. When we try not to do wrong, we do.

It's essential to be around Godly people for accountability and to be trained by their example. You can't do this on your own. When you get twisted over a pop-up from the pit, or react in the flesh, you need reminders that flesh against flesh doesn't work, misery demands company, and freedom isn't free.

When Jesus climbed the cross to die for your sins, the power of sin over you died with him. You're the beloved of Jesus, and you're worthy to embrace his Spirit within you.

Lord, I'm overwhelmed that your blood wiped my slate clean. I pray I will embrace your invitation for liberation from the enemy's concentration camp. Amen.

ROMANS 7:17-20, 8:1-6

Sounding Impressive

A comprehensive, fascinating exploration of the familial influences which are the bits and pieces of your spiritual foundation will give you a compelling, masterful account of the ongoing conviction of God's Spirit in your life. When checking out God's amazing fruit in your life because of special people speaking life over and into you, the Father reveals his master plan for you. Empowered by his Spirit, you dare call the creator of the universe *Abba, Father.*

Oh, how your pride and ego love to sound impressive with words that vibrate with cleverness, even when no one has a clue what they mean. You're saved by grace, not by anything you say or do. The Gospel truth will radically change all you've thought or known.

Dare to explore the preaching behind the teaching: the Shepherd always leads you to a place you can't go on your own. Your brokenness was a blessing because it got you to choose to follow Jesus.

Lord, thanks for revealing to me who I am in you. I pray I will stay in the middle of the sheepfold because the wolves devour those on the outside. Amen.

2 CORINTHIANS 3:17; JOHN 10:27

Faith Builders

It's imperative to have people speaking life and encouragement into you, and to run from those who speak death and condemnation. The tongue has the power of life and death. Jesus doesn't desire religion; he invites you to have an intimate, personal relationship with him.

Relationships are the key to your recovery. You can't elevate higher than the company you keep. Be on guard against those who influence your behavior. You need accountability, not a band-aid. To be in position where God desires you, keep company with faith builders who live in freedom. They will strengthen you when you're unsteady.

Constantly remind yourself that it's an inside job. Ask God to remove the dungeon the enemy constructed deep within you— the dark underground prison you thought you deserved. The Holy Spirit will close down the submerged, subterranean place of betrayal, hate, and offense, and refill the once bottomless, underground chamber of mental and physical suffering with his fruit: love, joy, peace, patience, kindness, goodness, faithfulness, gentleness, and self-control.

Lord, I pray I will love life and eat its good fruit. Thanks for removing my agony and misery and repairing the lacerations of my damaged heart. Amen.

PROVERBS 18:21; 1 CORINTHIANS 15:33; GALATIANS 5:22-23

Embrace the Love

It's essential to receive God's truth—walk in his light with other believers. Embrace how tenderly your sins have been erased by Jesus' cleansing blood. The actions of others encourage you to receive the unfathomable love Abba Father has. This is unfamiliar territory: you've judged yourself more harshly than anyone else ever could. God's love through others reaches into your once dead and hardened heart to extract your newly discovered love of Jesus and self.

As you grow to trust that God could love someone like you, his truth battles through the flesh and the enemy's lies. God has never given up on you. He ruthlessly and aggressively pursues your heart because he desires one-on-one fellowship.

Remember, even though you didn't know God personally at the time, he still saved you from the pit of hell. You'd been misinformed about who God truly was by other misinformed people. God is love, and the blood of his Son saved you. Be thankful.

Lord, I pray to be a person of God and receive your mercy.
I love your compassionate tenderness, in spite of my past. Amen.

1 JOHN 1:7; 1 CORINTHIANS 13:7; 1 PETER 2:10

Have a Great Day

Your recovery is about progress, not perfection. It's about being okay with taking the next step forward, doing the next right thing, and being at the next right place. It doesn't matter who comes against you or what circumstance arrives unexpectedly. You can have a great day even when bad things happen during the day. God honors your effort by the manifestation of his power in and through you. After all you've been through, you shouldn't be here; yet the Father gave you another opportunity.

God's greater than you and he is for you. This gives you hope and courage to look beyond any circumstance. This isn't about *if* circumstances come, it's about *when* they come. Don't be surprised or quickly twisted. Look on them as an opportunity, not an inconvenience. In addiction you were extremely inconvenient.

Now is your time to give everything to God. Get ready; it's coming!

Lord, I'm grateful you desire for me to remain in your love. I pray for strength to do the next right thing without over-thinking or complaining. Amen.

ROMANS 8:31; JOHN 15:9

Resentment Destroys Recovery

Your deep levels of feeling resentment, rethinking past negative thoughts, and rehearsing past hurts create a smokescreen from the pit of hell to cover up your fear, anger, and blaming others for your shame. You agreed with the devil's deceitful trick of suggesting you were paralyzed, panic stricken, paranoid, and a miserable failure. Hurtful words defined you, and fear kept you feeling alone, unlovable, and uncared for. Medicating that pain seemed the only option.

Fear declares: "I'm afraid and alone." Anger jumps in: "I'm mad, it's wrong, and I will never talk to that person again!" Confusion adds, "I messed up, I can't ever do anything right." Hurt says, "I trusted and was betrayed." Shame mumbles, "I'm disgraced, embarrassed, and full of regret." And silence arrives. *Nothing matters. I'll retreat and shut down.*

As you trust less and less, you shut down more and more— locked up tight in the prison where the enemy said you'd be safe. God sends fishermen to catch you and bring you back to him. They will teach you to draw near to God. Listen to them.

Lord, thanks for sprinkling my heart to cleanse my guilty conscience and washing my body clean with pure, living water. I pray I will listen to the fishermen you send, so I learn more about you.

Jeremiah 16:16; Hebrews 10:23

Self-Control and Perseverance

Self-control and perseverance are the tools to remain desperate in pursuing recovery, regardless of difficulty or opposition. You're worthy of a new life with Jesus where your past is forgiven, your present is fulfilling, and your future is secure. No one starts recovery on a winning streak. God allowed the storms of life to blow you into recovery, to hear his still quiet voice: "You're my beloved." In brokenness, sick and tired of yourself, you admitted your way wasn't working and you needed the Lord to guide you in his truth. You asked him to teach you, and with child-like faith, you placed your hope in him.

To wait on God seems a daunting task. The flesh demands instant gratification and throws a hissy-fit if it doesn't get what it wants. The challenge is to get in the present moment, the best you can, and pray to accept the things you can't change.

More of God, less of you. God's timing, not yours. He is working constantly on your behalf, taking no time-outs. Wait patiently. The Father's love will transform a hectic day into a restful, peaceful day.

Lord, thanks for remembering me according to your love, for you are good. I pray I will stick and stay this day until my head hits the pillow. Amen.

2 PETER 1:5-7; PSALMS 25:5, 7, 37:7

Kneeling to Pride

Pride's a big reason you don't appreciate others. When life is all about you, you don't value others for what they do, and you have no clue what others do for you. You push people away because you don't trust them, and then you wonder why they don't come around anymore. Pride will never admit to being wrong.

When absorbed with yourself, you ignore who God is and what he desires to do through you. The final result is a dead end—and possibly another relapse. When you admit you're stubborn, headstrong, bullheaded, and in dire need of God's grace and mercy, your pride lessens.

God didn't create robots: he desires that you choose to worship him. Your flesh is in conflict with his Spirit. Get up from kneeling to pride and run to kneel at Jesus' cross.

Lord, I pray I will seek counsel and be open to correction. I pray for courage not to bow down, kneel, and worship the idol of pride and control. I desire to kneel to you. Amen.

ROMANS 8:7; GALATIANS 5:17

First Look in the Mirror

It's easy to give God everything when you have nothing.
Recovery gives you an opportunity to leave the distractions and
chaos of the outside world, and work to get your inside world
put right. When your heart is in the right place, you'll see God
working on the outside.

Your first serious look at yourself in the mirror can be
frightening: you might be full of fear, anger, resentment,
unforgiveness, or lacking self-worth. Don't get upset at the
mirror. You're okay. Admitting you're poor in spirit is a huge
step forward. Submission and obedience are key to recovery. If
you are still calling the shots, you'll find yourself in big trouble.

Although you've made mistakes, God says you're not a mistake.
The Father loved you so much that he gave his Son to die for
you. Your new life deserves quick action. It's critical to respond
promptly when God reveals exactly what he desires from you.
Don't hesitate!

Lord, I pray for character that will sustain my recovery. I praise
you for how far you've brought me from the day I first looked in the
mirror. Amen.

MATTHEW 5:8; 1 SAMUEL 15:22; EPHESIANS 2:4-6

Line Up

Accountability plays a key role in recovery. God brings people into your life who can't be fooled or manipulated. When you admit you don't have a clue, it opens the door for God to come in.

Drugs, alcohol, and gambling may be gone, but without a new heart you'll continue to respond in the flesh. God searches and examines your heart and mind. Only he can touch your heart and remove strongholds.

The Lord desires you to respect, follow, love, and serve him with all your heart, so it's essential to get your heart work done. Your new life is deserving of quick and prompt action. You want to line up with God. He already knows about your circumstances. When you're overwhelmed, let the Holy Spirit overwhelm you instead with his glory. He can lift sickness, weakness, resentments, failure, and regret off your shoulders if you ask.

Lord, I pray you will send people after your heart into my life for accountability. I desire to quickly and promptly address issues in my life, so I can release them to you. Amen.

JEREMIAH 17:9-10; DEUTERONOMY 10:12

Lose It to Find It

Your greatest act of worship to God is to take everything you do and receive and embrace what he has for you—one day at a time. With radical trust, you can place your circumstances in God's hands, as he creates a pure heart and renews his steadfast Spirit within you.

Your desire to hear God's whisper of truth, rather than entertaining the enemy's lie, will be honored. It's when your mind starts throwing a fit of self-pity that the connection gets blocked. God's promises of protection and victory are your personal bodyguards to shield you. Jesus reveals himself in the Word, your faith gives you courage to act, and his Spirit empowers you to receive.

You begin to see with spiritual eyes what's going on around you; you no longer believe what your physical eyes see. There's absolutely no reason to try to figure out how God works, simply because you can't. It's your time to pursue the priceless treasure—Jesus—and walk into your new life.

Lord, I pray I will see what's going on around me through your glasses. I pray you continue the work you've begun in my heart. Bring it to completion. Amen.

PSALM 51:10; PROVERBS 2:7; MATTHEW 16:25

Spiritual Warfare Is Real

You need to know the enemy of your soul engages in spiritual warfare to take you out of recovery, and set you back into the abyss of addiction. It's his plan to steal your birthright. Jesus came that you might have a better life than you could ever have possibly imagined.

Soldiers are trained for situations where they and their fellow brothers-in-arms are placed in jeopardy. Their loyalty is displayed by action, not words. There's no room for pride, ego, or victims, on the spiritual battlefield. Engaging in hand-to-hand combat against spiritual strongholds with a plastic fork will fail. Your endless excuses not to fight with God's weapons will set you up to be captured, tortured, and killed by the enemy.

Elite armed forces expend all effort to bring a fallen buddy home, exhibiting great love that shows they would lay down their lives for others. Jesus died, in battle, for you to come home to him. Will you die to yourself for the one who died for you?

Lord, I pray for the safety of the armed forces, for those who set aside everything to help others. I thank you for the soldiers-in-Christ who surround me and help protect me from the enemy. Amen.

JOHN 10:10, 15:3; PROVERBS 17:17

Believe and Experience Fully

As you draw nearer to God, and experience his peace and presence, you want more one-on-one time with him. He will expose what you need to work on. Trust in him and go all in. With reckless abandon, push through the secrets you've held for so long.

An essential piece of your recovery puzzle is to seek God's grace to lift you from isolation, depression, shame, and guilt. When you admit your shortcomings, God is faithful and just to forgive you. He will put you back in right standing with him.

There's a stark difference between believing and experiencing. You can *believe* God removes all past transgressions, but when you *experience* it, you're taken to the next level. When the world says give up, hope says try it one more time. Don't quit. Be around champions who believe and experience the intensity of God's love. They can teach you to run to him rather than to addiction. God restores to you the joy of being saved.

Lord, I thirst to not just believe, but experience you fully. I pray for grace when I'm ready to give up. Help me try one more time. Amen.

1 JOHN 1:9; PSALM 51:12

Know the Father

Your addiction tested every relationship you were in, and past actions caused much pain. The important people in your life want to see the fruits of your new life in action. They don't want empty words and more broken promises.

The enemy is always in the grandstand, clapping and cheering for you to burn bridges. Be encouraged; God is all about relationships. When you seek him first, everything will fall into place in his timing.

Your battle is not against another person. It's against principalities of darkness. You're going to give in to something; it might as well be God. He can renew your mind and strengthen you. God sent his Son to purchase your freedom so he could adopt you as his child. When you draw near the Father, he will teach you how to be like him and no longer burn the bridges to your loved ones.

Lord, I praise you. I call out to you Abba Father. I pray I will love others as you love me—unconditionally. I'm grateful I'm one of your kids. Amen.

GALATIANS 4:3-7

Get to Your Feet

Many struggle with believing in the unseen and wonder if they even have a future. In the battlefield of your mind, you exhaust yourself trying to be worthy of God's love. Under your own power and doing it your way, you'll always fall short.

At a young age, the actions of adults in your life may have been different than how they told you to act—a double standard. People may have talked about God without really knowing him, setting up conflicts within you. *Have I done enough? Am I going to heaven? God can't love me.*

God says, "Get to your feet." He appointed you as his servant and witness to tell others still lost in addiction that there's hope. The future is secure. God set you apart and rescued you to rescue others. There's absolutely nothing you've done to disqualify yourself from this glorious mission. In fact, God enjoys showing off through those once considered foolish or powerless. It's powerful evidence of his presence.

Lord, I pray I will open my spiritual eyes to glance into the invisible until it becomes visible. Please remind me, if it's not about you, it won't work. Amen.

ACTS 26:16; 1 CORINTHIANS 1:26-27

A Shepherd Boy

When you can't wait for the day to be over, you're operating in your own strength. Your power will not keep you from worrying, entertaining anxiety, or participating in confusion. You're distracted from the truth that says, "This is the day the Lord has made; be glad!"

God equips you to have a great day, so you can replace an ordinary day with God's extraordinary one. Fear wants you to run to where you think you are safe. But there you only find yourself in a dark room with your knees under your chin.

God needs one person to start something amazing—like David. He was a young boy who stepped forward to fight the giant Goliath. God needs you step out and face off against your giants of fear and doubt. Every attack you've appropriately handled is another weapon in your arsenal. God can remove your giants if you seek him.

Lord, I pray for courage to cut off the heads of the giants in my life.
I pray for strength to grab your sword and fight. Amen.

1 SAMUEL 17:10-51

God's Spontaneous Love

In recovery, you learn the Father's law can be summed up by one command, "Love God, and love each other." Embracing this truth, you begin to enter the unfamiliar territory of learning to love yourself.

An example of his vast, unfathomable love is protecting and bringing you through the open door of opportunity to choose him to save your life. As you receive the Father's love, with child-like faith, and love others, his love within you grows ever stronger.

Only God can take you to the place where you learn more about him. The enemy tries to distract you from getting there, and your flesh absolutely doesn't want to go there. This can't be explained in the busy intellect of a self-proclaimed philosopher. You won't discover love while in the flesh or in the mind. Love springs up in you because of God's love for you. When you practice the Father's love with people you don't like, or can't stand, his love within you grows stronger.

Lord, thanks for telling me I am of great value to you, worthy of your love. When your Spirit fills my heart with love, I pray I will share it. Amen.

GALATIANS 5:14-15; 1 JOHN 4:12; ROMANS 5:5

Expectations of God

The resurrected Christ released you from the existence of doubt, hopelessness, and unbelief to bring you into his presence where faith and hope abound.

God is not moved by your need—he moves because of his love for you. God reached down and saved you while you were drifting in the sea of shame and fear and clinging to a small piece of your life. It was easy to pray because God was all you had left. Yet, he honored your faith and gave special favor.

Faith generates miracles, while doubt encourages tragedy. The only thing different from yesterday is your faith. As your confidence in God bursts forth from deep within you, his living Word is activated in and through you. Whatever God speaks, he acts; whatever he promises, he does. He doesn't change his mind, and he never lies. Don't have high expectations of others, but low expectations of God. Remove the limitations you've placed on him!

Lord, thanks for the wisdom to know my journey is never bigger than you. I pray for your gift of special favor to live by your power. Amen.

Ephesians 2:8; Numbers 23:19; 1 Corinthians 4:20

Activate Gratitude

One of the most challenging prayers for anyone in recovery is, "Not my thoughts, but your thoughts, Lord." Spiritually, this comes against the numerous excuses and reasons for hanging onto past resentments which clog the channel to the throne room.

Unknowingly, resentment hinders the living Word from bestowing the blessings God has in store for you. He is waiting to release them to produce the fruit he desires you to have and share with others.

God's ways and thoughts are higher than yours, and his Word prospers whenever it falls on fertile ground. God is bigger than what you've ever done; he's greater than your past, present, and future. It's your season to seek him while you can find him, and call on him while he's near. Gratitude is great medicine for the soul. Gratitude allows you to change your heart and make it obedient to God in you. It clears your obstructed channel to the Father.

Lord, I'm grateful your thoughts are higher than mine. My mind gets crazy at times. I pray to be more aware of keeping my channel to you clear. Amen.

ISAIAH 55:6-9, 12

Truth Spoken Effectively

Truth spoken in criticism, or judgment, is totally ineffective. It takes you, and the person you're talking to, back into condemnation and shame. The devil magnifies what you've seen, heard, and touched in your life—sometimes even experiences that go back to your childhood. Truth is twisted into a lie.

Truth spoken in love is truly effective, for the Word that God speaks is alive and full of power, and it can slice and separate your flesh from God's Spirit within you. The Spirit gives life; the flesh counts for nothing. The words God speaks are full of the Spirit and life: of power, love, and self-discipline.

You've got to do the work in order to claim what God has already done for you. He gives you weapons to be successful. Ask Jesus to fight for you, study the Word to know the truth, and let the Spirit sort the lie and truth out for you.

Lord, I pray to speak the name of Jesus over my circumstance before it robs my day. I pray to speak truth effectively, in love, to others. Amen.

1 JOHN 1:1-2; HEBREWS 4:12; JOHN 8:32, 16:13; 2 TIMOTHY 1:7

The First Valentine

The heart is the center and seat of affection; there's always a tie, or close connection, between the spiritual and physical. When your spiritual heart becomes hardened and shuts down, your physical heart shows wear and tear. Being heartbroken by loss or grief can also reflect in the physical body.

During addiction, your heart grew cold and lost compassion. You shut down, isolated yourself, and maybe felt unsafe to go anywhere. You might have been paranoid when you did. Jesus promises that he who stands firm to the end will be saved.

It's your season to recover. As God's grace begins to flow into your life, his mercy is evident beyond the shadow of a doubt. Jesus gave his heart and allowed it to be pierced—literally bursting— for you. When you reached total brokenness, your tears began to soften your hardened heart and hope began to seep in. Jesus was the first valentine in history. He asks you to be his.

Lord, thanks for being the first valentine. I pray for strength to search for you with all my heart and soul—and to find you. Amen.

MATTHEW 24:12-14; REVELATION 3:15-16; DEUTERONOMY 4:29

Beautiful Brokenness

Are you worthy? Of course not! Yet, God declares your worthiness and urges you to live a life worthy of the calling you've received. He invites you to receive the blessings he's already set aside for you. God gives sufficient grace for you to live your life in peace and freedom. He blesses your eyes to see the supernatural and your ears to hear his promises.

God met you in your darkest place. He puts great value on the pain you experienced. Your pain is useful: it allows you to meet others in their pain.

God creates you from rock bottom to shape the world you walk. A teacup smashed into many pieces looks useless, but it's still a teacup. Much like a broken teacup glued and pieced together, God takes your bits and pieces of brokenness and makes something beautiful.

Once overwhelmed by brokenness, you're now overwhelmed by how God made your brokenness beautiful. Who saves? God! Who redeems? Jesus! Who speaks life? The Holy Spirit! God's incredible portion of prosperity and joy is too good to pass up.

Lord Jesus, thanks for loving me as the Father loved you. I'm grateful you can use my journey of pain to help others. I'm thankful my journey is never bigger than you. Amen.

Ephesians 4:1; Matthew 13:16; Isaiah 61:7

Throw the Stone

The Pharisees brought a woman caught in adultery to Jesus and demanded she be stoned in accordance with the Law. If Jesus said no, he would violate Moses' Law; if he said yes, he violated Roman Law. Jesus said, "If any of you is without sin, let him be the first to throw a stone at her." The older ones walked away first, followed by younger ones, until only the woman and Jesus remained.

Jesus asked the woman where everyone went. "Does no one condemn you?" And because no one did, Jesus said he wouldn't either. Then he told her to leave her life of sin.

You were accused by pointy fingers of judgment for past failures, wrongdoings, and sin. You may have believed the enemy's legalistic law which condemned you to a lifeless existence of medicating your pain. Because of this immense guilt, you likely judged others harshly and always had a stone in your hand to throw. When you dare, by God's grace, to admit you're just as guilty, Jesus says to you what he said to the woman. "Neither do I condemn you." Release the rock in your hand, and let it drop to the ground.

Lord, thanks for loving me so powerfully, even when I was a hypocrite. I'm so grateful you don't condemn me. I desire to follow you and no longer walk in darkness. Amen.

JOHN 3:16, 8:3-12

The Father Delights in You

The busyness of the world, circumstances of the day, pop-ups from the past, regret, resentments, and times of testing violently shake your tree and disturb your peace. God's peace transcends all understanding. The blessing about distress is it gets you down on your knees crying out to the Lord—your rock and deliverer.

The hangman's noose was around your throat; waters rushed over you. Hell's ropes clinched you tight; death traps barred every exit. But God delivered you, and you're still here!

David wrote psalms to celebrate when the Lord delivered him from all his enemies. In response to David's cry for help, God came roaring out of heaven, reached down, took hold of him, and rescued him. Why? Because God delighted in him.

Under pressure by the tests you're facing today, God's giving you an opportunity to grow in perseverance and endurance. If you need deliverance from temptation or trial, call on God. He will respond because the he delights in you.

Lord, I pray you will keep my lamp burning, and turn my darkness into light. I praise you for the many times you've responded to my cries and delivered me. Amen.

Philippians 4:7; Psalm 18:3-19; James 1:2-3

Feeling Inadequate

In recovery, you become aware of the many times you felt crippled by feeling inadequate. No one enters recovery as a champion, and most likely you came in with no rest. You may have been harassed at every turn, with conflicts on the outside and fear within.

The story of Mephibosheth is your story. His grandfather Saul had tried, for years, to kill David. After David was King, he asked if any relatives of Saul had survived. Jonathan's son, Mephibosheth, was living. He was crippled in both feet at five years old. Unnoticed for years, he was called to the palace, and understandably feared for his life. He bowed before King David: "What is your servant, that you should notice a dead dog like me?" King David showed God's kindness to the son of his friend, Jonathan, and restored all of Saul's land to him. David invited him to always eat at his table.

God's in the reconciliation business, and he calls you to eat at his banquet table. The King of kings wants to restore a life of abundance to you. No longer crippled, you're the beloved of the King.

Lord, I praise you for your invitation to dine with you for eternity. Thanks for showing compassion and mercy to this once dead dog. Amen.

2 CORINTHIANS 7:5; 2 SAMUEL 9:3-10

Chutzpah: Jesus Is Able

Confidence can be defined as firmly believing, trusting, or having faith. The Yiddish word *chutzpah* means having a high level of self-confidence. Take captive the idea of quitting your recovery and exchange it for completion: stick and stay. You can be confident that he who began a good work in you will carry it on.

Wondering if you can is ineffective. Give up your issues of resentment and unforgiveness, and have the chutzpah to know Jesus is able. He has overcome the world. The counterfeit for confidence is a swindler who persuades his victims to trust him. The devil is out to steal, kill, and destroy the very assignment God has for you. He can disguise himself as an angel of light, so he appears as a trusted, godly servant. He gains your confidence, and then distorts the truth.

God is the solution. He cancels all the charges against you, and nails them to the cross. Through Jesus, you have been set free!

Lord, I pray I will say yes when you whisper. I trust you. I pray for chutzpah to choose you over entertaining the swindler. Amen.

PHILIPPIANS 1:6; JOHN 14:1, 16:33; COLOSSIANS 2:13-14; ROMANS 8:2

The Crusader's Dream

In a dream, the crusader entered the castle's chapel and noticed a person seated in the last row lifting his arms toward heaven. He continued to the altar, where a few candles provided a small amount of light, laid down on the floor, and prayed: "I Am, I present myself to you, to do with as you will." As tears began to flow, the crusader felt the stranger's hand upon his shoulder. A sweet aroma flowed throughout the chapel as the stranger began to speak softly.

"My beloved crusader, I've heard your plea for mercy and I accept your cry for grace; you are now mine. I'm taking you captive. I need you to tell others about me. I'll breathe life into you, give you words to speak, and teach you my ways. You'll drink from the wellspring of life."

As the crusader turned to see the stranger's face, he awoke and looked about to see where he was. He could smell the sweet aroma permeating throughout the room: peace, surpassing all understanding, came over him, and as he laid his head on the pillow, he fell into a blissful rest.

Lord, grant me strength to let go of the was, give me grace to live in the is, and renew my dreams for the is to come. Amen.

Not If, but When

The amazing, never-ceasing love of God is not something you can earn. If it were, you'd be striving to qualify for his love, and you'd fall short every time. God's unconditional love allows you to receive it and pray, "Lord, less of me, and more of you."

Your flesh throws a hissy-fit: it says things like *never* and *can't*. With child-like faith, you dare to stay and fight. You take captive every thought to make it obedient to Christ; you rebuke the devil in the name of Jesus. Scripture demolishes every argument of doubt and inability. You can exchange *I can't* for *I can through Christ.*

The flesh will always be with you, but it doesn't have to call the shots. The enemy isn't going to give you free reign, but you don't need to believe the lie. God's love gives you the courage needed to give up your past and let God sort it out for your good. The new you can't come out until the old you belongs to God.

Lord, I pray to activate my rescue with your Word. I'm grateful I don't have to understand how everything works in my mind. I pray to stay and fight. Amen.

2 CORINTHIANS 10:3-5; PHILIPPIANS 4:13; ROMANS 8:28

The Storm of Addiction

When hoping for peace and the storm of addiction threatens with fear and terror licking at your heels, press in. When the demand seems more than the supply, don't give up. The enemy screams, "You can't recover!" while God whispers, "You can!"

If you stay where you are, the terrible storm will continue to rage for days, blotting out the sun and stars until all hope is gone. Evaluate what's really going on and you'll see the purpose of your storm is to discover your only hope.

In the midst of the storm, take a deep breath and know whatever you're fighting is on the run. In a daring act of radical trust, you can step into God's grace because your hope is only in him. The storm will retreat, terror will slither away, and peace will flow in. The challenge is not to go back to where you were. Shake the dust off your sandals and go where God desires you to be.

I pray I will believe in the promises of my recovery. I pray to look at the solution not the problem. Amen.

JEREMIAH 8:15; ACTS 27:20; PSALM 39:7

Go through It to Get to It

Total brokenness brought you to the edge of the cliff, ready to leap. You were a shipwrecked ragamuffin: tattered, shabby, exhausted, beat-up, and worn down. God's tender mercy gave you courage to admit you're weak, your life is miserable, and your will got you into extremely ugly places. God's mercy gives you a new beginning. He called you, and saved you! Do you know you didn't save yourself?

Be grateful for the misery of your past, and don't be ashamed of all you went through to get to him! In fact, he waited for you; his patience gave you time to be saved. God chose you, called you, declared you not guilty, and promised you his glory.

Only God's Spirit in you knows what God's redeeming grace will do for you. This is progress, not perfection; it takes time to unlearn all the twisted thinking you once believed. Begin with this truth: if God is for you, no one can be against you.

I pray I will embrace being a ragged child. I pray for gratitude for all the misery I went through to get to you. Amen.

2 PETER 3:15; ROMANS 8:28-31

Reminders

You need people to stimulate and refresh your memory to stay the course when behaviors get a bit twisted. Your tender heart can be at risk of being hardened once again. Be grateful, not irritated, when your actions, or words, are confronted lovingly by someone who cares. They love you enough to remind you to leave your foolish ways behind.

Your reactions and words are the barometer of where you are in recovery. Can you admit when your thinking is twisted? God provides a lamp to light your way by strategically bringing along extraordinary people who encourage you to stay on point. They will give honest, wise advice.

As you seek counsel from those in your life who help save you from yourself, you no longer need someone to co-sign your addictive behavior or agree with your drama. Thank them for speaking, in love, the words that are difficult to hear.

Lord, I pray you will bless those who stimulate and refresh my memory when it's twisted. I'm thankful for those reminders even when I am having a good day. Amen.

2 Peter 3:1; Proverbs 6:23, 9:6

The Father's Love

The Father's love for all is radically demonstrated by his action of giving his Son to die for you while you were still in sin. The Father has hope and faith in you, shown by his love to you. Dare to embrace his greatest gift ever given. Take a deep breath and ignore your pride for a moment. Declare that you will not fall for the enemy's counterfeit love, and step into the faith the Father has freely given you.

In spite of your past experiences of life, whether self-inflicted or bad choices, the Father has a plan and purpose for you. The only thing still clinging on your tree after being so severely shaken by addiction is a tiny mustard seed of faith. That's his gift to you.

The bedrock of your new faith is in place for a confident, hopeful assurance that nothing can separate you from the Father's love but you. This is essential to your recovery: the Father is love. When you live in love, you live in the Father, and the Father lives in you.

Father, I pray for the power to understand how wide, how long, how high, and how deep your love for me is. Amen.

ROMANS 5:8, 8:28; JOHN 3:16; 1 JOHN 4:16; EPHESIANS 3:18

The Son's Love

God's Word speaks of understanding the Father's love. While you can experience this love, it's too great to understand fully. The Son's love will make you complete with the fullness and power that come from the Father.

Imagine the pain and brutality of the torture endured. Jesus was beaten and bloodied until you would scarcely know he was human. Only the Son would climb the cross to crush the sin brought into this world by the first human.

The Son became sin for you to become a saint—in right standing with the Father. The Son's action of walking through the violence of the cross was a glorious, masterful act of redemption. He strategically placed you smack dab in the middle of where he desires you to be. As you become empowered by his shed blood, a deeper relationship with the Son invites you to give yourself to him, as he gave himself to you.

Lord, I desire to be a cloud that has rain to refresh, and a tree that has abundant fruit. Help me to experience the Son's blood so I can be renewed and restored. Amen.

EPHESIANS 3:19; ISAIAH 43:27, 52:14; 2 CORINTHIANS 5:21

Once an Orphan

God hears an orphan's cry to be saved from the lie that addiction's the only way to medicate the pain deep inside. Your plan is a total disaster. God is eager to share his plan for you. He wants to adopt you as one of his children, and draw you into his family.

Children need an environment of love. They need to know God's promises give hope. God is a strong and trustworthy anchor. As a new babe in Christ, you need milk, not solid food. Be patient with the Father's timing; you'll learn it is perfect. You might ask the Father for the keys to the car, while still in diapers.

As an infant, grow in faith and trust. Don't get twisted when God says you need to grow up first. He desires to teach and train you. All must receive the kingdom of God like little children.

Lord, I need help to grow up. I pray to be willing to be spoon fed by you, even when I want to eat steak and potatoes by myself. Amen.

EPHESIANS 1:5; MATTHEW 6:33; HEBREWS 5:12; MARK 10:15

Discipline to Seek Him

Discipline begins after your life's tree is so severely shaken that all that remains is faith, hope, and love. What qualifies you to walk this path is his gift of faith—the confidence that what you hope for will actually happen. It gives you assurance about things you cannot see.

God's love protects you during this journey of trusting that his plan is better than yours. Seek first the kingdom of God. Make use of daily devotions, pray, and soak in the Scripture. As you seek him, you discover it's absolutely possible not to be anxious or fearful about tomorrow. You're in a different dimension of being in the present moment. It's as if a door opens to see God active and participating in your life every minute of every day.

The enemy's counterfeit for discipline is to let you believe that you're in control. The truth is that discipline is about seeking God to discover the gift of a solid recovery. Stop listening to what's going on between your ears!

Lord, I pray for the discipline to seek you first before my busy mind kicks in. I praise you for the gift of hope. Amen.

1 CORINTHIANS 13:13; HEBREWS 11:1; MATTHEW 6:33; EPHESIANS 5:17

The Upper Room

Jesus, the King of kings, began his radical revolution against the religious and worldly standards by becoming human and being a servant. The Son of God washing the feet of his disciples assaults our pride. When Jesus knelt down to wash those grubby feet, the seismic shift kicked the hypocritical-Pharisee-morality right out the door, defying man's way and glorifying the Father's way. He invites us to follow his example and wash one another's feet. Do you know your recovery depends on serving others?

Jesus even washed the feet of the one who would betray him. That's pretty powerful stuff! Your Savior came not for the self-righteous and religious people, but for the sinners, down-and-outers, black sheep, tax collectors, prostitutes, and ragged children.

The Lord makes righteous those pathetic, feeble, imperfect human beings who accepted him personally. The Messiah pursues you with his tender, compassionate, and merciful love, and prepares a place for you.

I pray I will follow your example and serve others in recovery. I'm grateful you are taking me to your upper room in heaven. Amen.

JOHN 13:5, 14, 14:2; LUKE 22:27

Stay

The key for recovery is patiently enduring testing and temptation. Each test endured becomes your testimony. You've tried for years, but weakness of character keeps rearing its ugly head, resulting in another detox, treatment, jail, and relapse. There's stuff in you that needs to be removed to stop this chaos and insanity. Get into Jesus' lap, and savor his protection. God has been patiently waiting, giving you time to be saved. Will you be patient with the one who is patient with you?

God took the pipe out of your hand, set the bottle down, and stopped a casino visit; dare to trust he won't leave you until he gives you everything he promised you.

God's Spirit encourages your participation on the pilgrimage to freedom. He is not slow; he's being patient for your sake, training you to receive what he has for you. Do you give a seven-year-old a car? Don't leave before the blessing!

I pray I will endure, patiently, so as to witness the "afterward."
I pray I will remain humble so I'm not humiliated. Amen.

JAMES 1:12; 2 PETER 3:15; GENESIS 28:15

His Living Water

Similar to a garden, your recovery experiences different seasons: prepare, seed, water, fertilize, and harvest. Without living water to nourish and empower your new life, recovery becomes limp and lifeless. The weeds of no accountability, self-centeredness, criticism, and laziness will result in no harvest. If you're lazy in recovery, you'll soon be back on the prison chain-gang working hard in a relapse. Are you aware the enemy is waiting for you in the church parking lot?

As a garden thirsting for water, Jesus says, "come to me and drink" while his grace and mercy provides the fertilizer for the harvest.

Whatever season you're in, you've been given the choice to embrace or let go, turn into or away, listen or speak, drink living water or remain thirsty, give up or keep going. God's Spirit empowers your recovery and encourages you not to become weary; do not give up so you will reap your harvest. It's your season!

Lord, I thirst for your living water and the courage to drink it. Help me get to my pillow tonight—clean and sober. Amen.

JOHN 4:10, 7:37; GALATIANS 6:9

Rebuilding or New Building?

Tornadoes leave a path of destruction, causing anguish and chaos for those affected. We've all seen pictures where the foundation is all that's left, and even that can be damaged.

Addiction has wiped out many homes, damaging relationships. The resulting guilt and shame produces much chaos and heartache. This is not rebuilding time; it's new building time. Are you willing to receive God's dumpster to start cleaning up the mess caused by the tornado of your past?

God is going to take you to places you've never been. By wisdom a house is built, and the great contractor, if asked, will construct your new house on a solid foundation, giving you a fresh start. Christ makes you a new creation; the old has gone, and the new has come! This is the deal of a lifetime: a new house of recovery, with rooms full of rare and beautiful treasures. Allow him to begin his good work in you.

Lord, I pray for the courage to stay out of the way. I desire to start cleaning up the mess of my addiction. Amen.

PROVERBS 24:3-4; 2 CORINTHIANS 5:17

Commitment

Evaluate exactly what you're committed to. You exhibited strong commitment in the past, but to the wrong things for the wrong reasons. You have it in you to stand your ground. The obstacles are the challenges you face. In addiction, you were all in. You can now use this to fully commit to your recovery.

When addiction became comfortable, you were forced to respond to the consequences; yet when it became miserable, dark, and dreary, you cried out, making a commitment to God with the words, "Help me, Lord. Save me! I'll do whatever it takes!" He wasted no time and saved you.

Only the Word of God in you reveals the practical application of his spiritual principles for your new life. Commit wholeheartedly to being confident that nothing you do for him is a waste of your time or effort. Commit to the one who saved you!

I pray for courage to commit to the things of God. In gratitude, I commit to the one who saved me. Amen.

1 CORINTHIANS 15:58

Declaring Poverty

After believing the lie that you're responsible for getting everything you want, God's promise seems a bit reckless. The pilgrimage to freedom begins by declaring your poverty. It's essential to leave your throne and kneel before his. Seek first the kingdom of God, and what appears impossible becomes a possibility. Choose another day of recovery rather than relapse. Do you dare believe recovery is possible for you?

Circumstances can seem unbearable when thoughts of the liquor store, drug dealer, or casino begin creeping in from the darkness. Yet, the Holy Spirit's gentle whisper speaks life. *You can't do it, but God can.*

By God's grace and mercy, you can step away from the creeping darkness into his light—a light so bright you need special-order Son-glasses. Climb into his lap to rest and receive his gift of everything you need for your recovery today.

Lord, I pray I will seek you first above all else. I pray to believe my recovery is possible even when it seems impossible. Amen.

MATTHEW 6:33, 19:26; MARK 9:23

Saved by Grace

It's not anything you did to step out of addiction and into God's unique witness-protection program. You hit rock bottom while hanging on to the enemy's ticket of despair, drowning in a vast ocean, clinging to a piece of life's wreckage with sharks circling about. There is absolutely nothing on this planet that could have saved you but God. His hand lifted you from disaster, and strategically placed you into a program of faith, hope, and love. He set your feet on a firm place.

God's truth reveals your four choices—jail, mental institutions, death, or recovery. You might as well give recovery a shot—the other three will always be waiting! It's an absolute blessing to discover God has a purpose for your life—to save others in addiction.

Your recovery depends upon reaping what you sow; and you can't keep what you have unless you give it away! This day, you don't want justice—you want mercy!

Lord, thanks for the mercy shown to me. I ask for the courage to participate in God's grace for my life. Amen.

PSALMS 37:24, 40:2

Don't Quit

Upon accepting your life is one of disorder and the only way is God, the mist lifts a bit and the sun breaks through the clouds. You've believed the lie that your thinking, plans, and actions are the only way to repair the broken bridges and get back all you lost. God tenderly, mercifully, makes a way and a path through your most challenging circumstances. Do you believe God is a man of his Word?

God desires you to see from his perspective and cancel your long-time reserved seat on the emotional roller coaster of decisions.

Know that God hasn't left you, and he will protect you. Dare to push the recovery reset button—the light from heaven is about to break upon you. Don't quit!

Lord, I'm grateful you won't quit until you give me everything you promise if I don't quit. Amen.

ISAIAH 43:16; GENESIS 28:15; LUKE 1:78

Maintain Your Recovery

God's still, quiet voice says, "Stop trying to control your use of alcohol, drugs, or gambling, because it never works. You're not able to plan your course!" Your best thinking got you into treatment, jail, or prison. That's far less than what God has for you. He didn't design you to be in control of your life or your recovery.

Be on guard because your addictive behavior remains alive in you, insisting on doing things its way. Only God can keep you in perfect peace when your thoughts are fixed on him!

The twisted thinking in the battlefield of the mind reveals the lack of control you actually have—words say you love someone; yet, actions say you don't. The peace God leaves with you protects you from trouble, anxiety, and fear. Trust that his perfect peace covers you.

I pray for courage to maintain my recovery. I pray for all fear to be gone and peace to take its place. Amen.

PSALM 31:14; ISAIAH 26:3; JOHN 14:27

Can You Stay Committed?

It's essential to remember entering recovery powerless, beaten down, and not on a winning streak, yet, your past never disqualified you from God's love. His invitation is to participate in his plans for the good things he planned for you long ago.

When you're part of God's plan, your plans change, and you no longer need to live below your privileges as one of his kids. Take a deep breath, and commit your recovery to the Lord.

God knows the future. His plans will prevail. Past attempts to find love, joy, and peace ended in failure. Get to know the one who can give you all of those things! When you commit to God's plan of recovery and find his purpose for your life, you will experience freedom from addiction.

Lord, I pray for courage to go where your path leads me. I pray for strength to commit to the plans you have for me and to finish strong. Amen.

EPHESIANS 2:10; PROVERBS 16:3; JEREMIAH 10:23

Absolute Surrender

Get out of that busy mind. No more hissy-fits about losing control, or expecting peace to come through circumstances or possessions. God is not the great I *was*, or *should have been*—he's the Great I *Am*. It doesn't matter where you've been, or what you've gone through; it's all about where God is taking you.

Only in God's timing does he release his blessings to you—the Lord waits to be gracious, and blesses those who wait for him. In fact, you thought the blessing was what you were waiting for; however, the blessing comes during the wait. We submitted to our addiction for years; why not try recovery and wait on God?

I surrender to you, heavenly Father. I desire to wait on you and love your mercy. Amen.

JOB 22:21; ISAIAH 30:18

A Living Problem

You failed God, but he didn't fail you. He not only rescued you, but God will place people in your life to guide you to freedom. You had issues before addiction—that's what you medicated. Recovery allows you to address the why behind the what.

The blessing is that you didn't get what you deserved. God did not ignore your prayer and lifted you out of the dirt and miry clay. You no longer need to be isolated. Do you really believe you can recover on your own?

Recovery is the lighthouse for those shipwrecked during the violent, destructive storms of life—abuse, abandonment, betrayal, fear, disrespect, and resentment. These strongholds in the secret, dark places in you can now be brought into his healing light. When you admit you're weak and poor, God strengthens you. His power rests on you. Go for it; it's your turn!

I pray for strength in times of weakness. I pray for wisdom to know the why behind the what of my addiction. I praise you for another chance to recover, even when I throw a fit because it seems hard. Amen.

Exodus 20:2; Psalm 66:20; 2 Corinthians 12:9

Ask for Advice

Your pride keeps plans secret because of shame. A constant war rages between your ears, where flesh engages in mortal combat against spirit. It's an active armed conflict, designed by the thief, to steal, kill, and destroy you. Jesus has already won the war by his sacrifice on the cross so you may have life, yet the battle for your soul continues.

When you admit you're not able to plan your own course, recovery depends upon you not going to war without counsel. Do you believe you must seek advice before making decisions?

God will guide you through what he brought you to! The enemy twisted you to think you had all the answers, but seeking advice for your plans helps limit rash, emotional decisions—which bite you later. Your flesh hates spiritual advice, and the enemy says you don't need counsel from others. To recover, God's way is the only way!

I pray to seek counsel and advice before making decisions.
I know a different perspective could save my life. Amen.

PROVERBS 20:18; JOHN 10:10; JEREMIAH 10:23

His Hands and Feet

A daily check-up on the condition of your heart is significant. A good-hearted person who hears God's message will cling to it, no matter what the circumstance, and produce a huge harvest. His Word protects you from enemy attacks of fear, depression, doubt, and the subtle critical spirit searching for a place to roost. Cling to the Lord's strength.

In the flesh, you're clueless and self-absorbed. In the Spirit, you help others because you were once helped. Can someone else become more important than you?

God has other lost sheep in need of help to escape their darkest day. As you watch God's hand reach out with a love that knows no boundary and pull another ragged child from their lifeless existence, you suddenly realize it's your hand becoming the hand of Jesus. Have courage to be his hands and feet. The workers are few for the great harvest. God will bless those who bless others!

I pray I will cling to, and take refuge in, God's Word. I desire for God's hand to reach out through mine to help another addict. Amen.

LUKE 8:15; MATTHEW 9:37

Refresh Your Memory

You need someone in your life to let you know when your actions put your soft, tender heart at risk of becoming hardened. Someone who will stimulate your wholesome thinking and refresh your memory. The enemy is always working to create division with those God has strategically placed in your life.

When your behavior is confronted, the response is typically defensive with denial, excuses, or reasons. The right response is gratitude that someone cares enough to let you know there's danger ahead. Do you get upset when hearing a reminder from a godly person?

Your reactions are a true barometer of where your recovery is. You need people who are a lamp to light the way ahead of you. Real faith is evident by actions fueled with wisdom and truth, not foolishness and excuses. To recover into freedom, stay away from those who co-sign your behavior by telling you what you want to hear. Jesus asks you to learn from him and find rest for your soul.

I pray I will listen to those who light the way with correction.
I desire to stand firm in the truth. Amen.

2 PETER 3:1; PROVERBS 6:23; MATTHEW 11:29

My Plans? His Purpose!

In spite of our great plans, the Lord's purpose always prevails. You can be grateful for the plans made which didn't work out, as addiction never allowed contentment. Chaos, guilt, and shame ruled the day, greasing the skids to lonely, dark places. Everything you've experienced—anxiety, depression, guilt, regret, abuse, and shame—has been turned by God to work for your good. Do you accept God's purpose for you is to be free of addiction?

God is using the past to get you to where he desires you to be this day. Be grateful you're alive. Your focus is to remain steadfast in recovery even when playing in the mud seems the way to go. The tiny seed God planted in you while in your mother's womb is ready to harvest; your tests now become a testimony.

The evil, violent storm of addiction scattered your life's puzzle pieces helter-skelter. God has diligently recovered all your broken and dislocated pieces—to properly fix and fit together in his beautiful tapestry of a new, blessed, abundant life.

I'm grateful God is working out everything for my good, and I'm thankful God's purpose will prevail over my many plans. Amen.

PROVERBS 19:21; ROMANS 8:28; COLOSSIANS 1:20

Our Purpose

Let's be clear, God's purpose for you is not to be an addict. His truth says you have only one purpose—to worship him forever. God desires your time, talent, and tithe. Only God can fill the emptiness you've been medicating for relief from pain. He provides your needs to overflowing, while his love always protects and perseveres. Do you believe the rest of your life can be the best of your life?

You learn the principle of purpose in your life by hanging out with people of purpose. Observe their deeds, love, faith, service, and perseverance. It's extremely difficult to measure yourself in the midst of a trial or storm, so ask people of love, faith, and service how your recovery program is looking to them.

Worship God, and his living water will flow through you to others. Continue to do more than when you first came into recovery.

I pray to focus upon my purpose—to worship God. I pray perseverance will finish its work in me one day at a time. Amen.

JEREMIAH 32:29; 1 CORINTHIANS 13:7; REVELATION 2:19

St Patrick's Day

In one of two surviving papers written by St. Patrick, he writes of the daily spiritual warfare battling the pagan druids, hostile chieftains, and murderous kings. He endured extreme hardships preaching to and baptizing the Irish in the name of the Father, Son, and Holy Spirit.

God's presence is guaranteed by the death and resurrection of Jesus and it is your defense against the evil within you and the evil outside of you. No weapon used against you will defeat you. Put on God's armor, and resist the enemy, so after the battle, you'll be standing firm.

Lord, I'm grateful that your presence surrounds me. I'm thankful your Spirit identifies the enemy for me. Amen.

Romans 8:7; Ephesians 6:12-13

Place of Safety

Your incessant intellectual thoughts rolling through the busy battlefield of your mind paints a drab picture. In the flesh, life is colorless and insecure; in the Spirit, the rainbow-like colors are a reflection of our Father's refuge. This isn't about your train running on time; it's about being willing to ride his bus and rest in him.

God will never lead you to where he won't sustain you, and he gives you the desire to obey him and the power to do what pleases him. Do you rest in Jesus' lap?

God delivers you through the dark night of raging storms, the violence of hurricane winds, and the intense, severe thunderstorms, to the first gleam of dawn, bursting forth into his light of a new day. Many times in recovery, the blessings come after suffering. Triumph comes because you endured. Trust that God's glory is on the other side of any test or adversity.

I pray to ride God's bus without telling him where to go. I'm grateful to rest in Jesus' lap. I believe joy comes in the morning. Amen.

DEUTERONOMY 33:27; PHILIPPIANS 2:13; PROVERBS 4:18; ROMANS 8:28

His Perfect Love

Fear is false evidence appearing real. It's the enemy's trick for you to believe God's love is imperfect and conditional. The truth is that God's love prevented you from getting what you deserved. Although you failed him, he didn't fail you. God heard your prayer, never withdrew his unfailing love from you, cast out fear, and unlocked your prison door. Are you willing to receive his perfect love?

Your challenge is to embrace his perfect timing: his schedule, leading, path, direction, grace, mercy, courage, love, and plan for your life. You have persevered and confronted your false self. Be encouraged to know the grace that got you into recovery is the same grace that sustains recovery.

The enemy twists you to think you can recover on your own—without any kind of accountability or encouragement. Keep watch and pray.

I thank you, Father, for loving me in spite of me. I pray your Spirit empowers me to seek you first and not grow weary. Amen.

1 JOHN 4:18; PSALM 66:20; REVELATION 2:3; MATTHEW 26:41

The Father of Faith

God changed Abram's name to Abraham because of his great faith. He knew that God could do anything he promised. This call to faith means you're no longer on a ship with no name, in the middle of a vast ocean, being tossed about during a violent storm. God gently requests you to allow him to do for you what you absolutely cannot do for yourself. God saved you. Have a bit of faith that he will bring you into freedom. Do you believe he can?

Let's be real. There will be worries, frustrations, fear, guilt, and shame coming at you; this means you're on the right track. You no longer need to be the person everyone has to deal with, or drain and exhaust everyone around you. God can turn the worst of the worst into the best of the best.

How much faith, this day, is needed to believe this? A tiny mustard seed of faith is all that's needed to say to any mountain standing before you, "Move!" and it will move.

I pray for courage, with faith like Abraham, to claim God's promise for my recovery. I only need a tiny mustard seed. Amen.

ROMANS 4:17,21; MATTHEW 17:20

Jesus' Assignment

Jesus knew the assignment his heavenly Father had entrusted to him. He would endure pain, shame, and suffering before being nailed to the cross. Jesus' life was lived to the glory of his Father, and his death, likewise. Your grief he took upon himself, your sorrows lifted onto his back, your sins he claimed as his own, your tears he wiped from your eyes. The true high priest, the perfect sacrificial lamb, the Lord of lords, offered his life so that you might have eternal life.

Jesus measured the oceans in the hollow of his hands; he was with God before the creation of the world. All things were made through him. Yet, he came in obedience to the Father to take the very punishment you deserved.

With reckless abandon and child-like faith, begin your journey to that special, quiet place of reflection where discernment, truth, clarity, and wisdom exist in abundance. It's only there where you'll discover your beloved Messiah's strength revealed by his actions because of his great love for you.

Lord, I place my hands into yours, to guide and lead me as we follow your footprints to Calvary. Amen.

HEBREWS 10:10; ISAIAH 40:12; JOHN 1:1-4

The Full Extent of His Love

Before the Passover celebration, Jesus knew his time had come. He showed the disciples the full extent of his love. He already knew the Father had given him authority over everything. He had come from God and would return to God. The King of kings began a radical revolution against the religious and worldly standards by the simple act of washing the feet of his disciples. He invited them to do the same.

The feelings of superiority, manipulating to sit at the head of the table, entitlement for special privileges, and the hypocritical Pharisee morality were kicked right out the door the moment Jesus kneeled. He came for you and me—the pathetic, feeble, imperfect human beings who admit to be sinners, lost, and in dire need of him.

The huge crowds who greeted Jesus on Palm Sunday when entering Jerusalem are long gone. It's now just you and the Christ Messiah. He whispers gently in your ear: "Go and wash someone's feet."

Lord, I pray to follow your example and be like a servant to others. Thanks for washing my feet with so much love and care. Amen.

JOHN 13:1-14; LUKE 22:26

The Garden

Gethsemane means *place of crushing*. The name comes from an olive press located there. Jesus came to the Garden to be crushed. The agony, horror, and deep distress he experienced was so humanly unbearable that he asked his Father if it were possible to avoid the suffering. In a glorious moment, he reaffirmed why he had come to earth as a human: he chose the Father's will over his own, and he did it for you.

Satan's incessant, unrelenting attacks against him were all lies: *How can one man do this? Do you really believe you can bear the full burden of sin? Saving their souls is too costly. No one, never, ever! Who is your Father?* All were attacks against God's plan of salvation and the very essence and identity of Jesus.

Jesus fell face down to the ground, and an angel from heaven came to strengthen him. He was in such agony of spirit his sweat fell to the ground as great drops of blood. Jesus' identity gives you a new identity in him.

Lord, I'm so touched by what you endured for me. I pray, by your grace, I will endure the devil's attacks against my new identity in you. Amen.

MARK 14:32-36; LUKE 22:43-44

Disfigured

Jesus committed no sin, neither was deceit found in his mouth. He was betrayed by one of his own, dragged for miles and beaten, to stand before the religious leaders and teachers of the Law. Caiaphas, the high priest, asked if Jesus claimed to be the Messiah. Jesus said he was. The room went ballistic: "He's guilty! Liar! He must die!" They spit, hit, and taunted Jesus as humiliating sarcasm flowed through their lips. Then they gave the Son of God over to the Romans.

Later, the human body of God's beloved Son had endured such physical beating and inhumane torture, he was disfigured and marred beyond human likeness.

Only with God's Spirit can you grasp the unfathomable depth of his unconditional, never-ending love. It's critical that you receive His sacrifice. Jesus died so you no longer go foolishly skipping through the enemy's minefield of addiction. It's time to look closely at the hits Jesus took for you, so you don't have to be tortured anymore. Make sure you don't spit on him.

Lord, your humility and willingness to complete your Father's assignment on my behalf, is incredible. I pray I will receive your gift of being born again—my true priceless treasure paid for with your blood. Amen.

1 Peter 2:22; Matthew 26; Isaiah 52:14

Pilgrimage to the Cross

Jesus, tortured and weak from loss of blood, carried his cross to Golgotha. He persevered to the destination where he took upon himself all our sins, shortcomings, and character defects. Each nail driven into his hands and feet, every insult yelled, and each gob of spit was ours. The soldiers threw dice for his garment. The first words of reverence spoken to Jesus since being taken prisoner was by a criminal next to him. His seed of faith knew Jesus had done nothing wrong, and his request to be remembered was honored.

Jesus cried out to his Father in anguish as he was forsaken. The light of the Son died, as the light of the sun darkened. God, being perfect and just, couldn't look at his Son because our sin was on him. In death, he was separated from his Father: the spiritual desolation of the darkness and silence more agonizing than the physical torture.

Joseph, Nicodemus, and others took Jesus' body and laid it in a tomb, sealed and guarded by Roman soldiers. The Pharisees thought the problem of Jesus was taken care of.

Lord, thanks for honoring your Father. I'm so grateful for your great love—to accept agonizing torture and die so that I might live. I'm humbled you endured separation from your Father for me. Amen.

LUKE 23

Day of Waiting

The religious leaders had manipulated the Roman Governor to condemn an innocent man who was a threat to the religious status quo and the Pharisee Temple Corporation. Dozens of witnesses saw Jesus' body lowered to the ground, placed in a grave carved in the rock, sealed by a large stone, and now guarded by an elite squad of Roman soldiers. The religious leaders had to be very pleased with how quickly they had removed the trouble-maker from their midst.

Jesus' tomb became God's workshop to undo the tragedy that had taken place in the Garden of Eden. He kept his promise spoken hundreds of years earlier. It was God's will that his Son die and lay in the grave to cover our sins.

Separated from his Father on our behalf, Jesus willingly carried out his assignment, meeting sin and death alone. Allow Jesus' blood to cleanse you. Rejoice that death has no more power over you.

Lord, what a stressful day of waiting for your disciples. With hope and expectancy, I await the morning light of your resurrection. I know the planet will rumble when daybreak arrives. Amen.

HOSEA 13:14

He Is Risen Indeed!

As the new day was dawning, Mary Magdalene and the other Mary went out to visit the tomb. Suddenly there was a great earthquake! For an angel of the Lord came down from heaven, rolled aside the stone, and sat on it. His face shone like lightning, and his clothing was as white as snow. The guards shook with fear when they saw him, and they fell into a dead faint. Then the angel spoke to the women. "Don't be afraid!" he said. "I know you are looking for Jesus, who was crucified. He isn't here! He is risen from the dead, just as he said would happen. Come, see where his body was lying. And now, go quickly and tell his disciples that he has risen from the dead, and he is going ahead of you to Galilee. You will see him there. Remember what I have told you."
The women ran quickly from the tomb. They were very frightened but also filled with great joy, and they rushed to give the disciples the angel's message. And as they went, Jesus met them and greeted them. And they ran to him, grasped his feet, and worshiped him.
(Matthew 28:1-9 NLT)

Grace now envelops the planet. Jesus destroyed death and brings life and immortality through his living Word; in other words, Jesus' Resurrection put death to death. In his blood is salvation, life, heavenly sweetness, strength of mind, and joy of spirit. Dare to participate in his way, his truth, and his life.

Lord, I pray, by grace, to live by faith in the Son of God, who loves, and gave himself for me. I pray for courage to take up my cross daily and follow you. Amen.

MATTHEW 28:1-10; 2 TIMOTHY 1:9-10; REVELATION 1:18; JOHN 14:6; GALATIANS 2:20

Restless or Restful?

Wired? Tense? Lack of energy? Anxious? Twisted? Distracted? Uptight? Double-minded? How long must you struggle with anguish in your soul, with sorrow in your heart? You might look good on the outside, but inside you're dying from lack of intimacy. At times, we all sit down and have tea with the enemy as he tricks us by numbing our minds with confusion. Behind the smile is the hot lava flow of anger waiting to erupt. Jesus tells us we can find rest in him.

You medicate pain with alcohol, drugs, gambling, eating, spending, hoarding, or something else. After all, everyone on this planet is in recovery from something. You isolate when feet are heavy, legs dragging, insides drying up by the intense heat of anxiety, and when depression calls, it's shut-down time.

You've searched for rest in all the wrong places. Only in the presence of the Shepherd do you find rest in green meadows; he leads you beside peaceful streams. God's promise of entering his rest still stands today!

Lord, I thank you for letting me rest in your lap. Today, I pray to make every effort to enter your rest. Amen.

PSALMS 13:2, 23:2; MATTHEW 11:28; HEBREWS 4:1

The Gate

As you learn more of the blessings God has for you, his still, quiet voice rises above the endless chatter between your ears. Faith allows you to tap into the radical concept that the God of all creation takes time to listen whenever you call on him and pray to him. As you seriously seek him with all your heart, you'll find him. As your trust in him deepens, the waters of life flow into the vast wasteland of your emptiness, transforming it into an oasis of refreshment.

Don't panic; God gave his Son to be the good shepherd to lead you. Jesus knows you and he laid his life down for you. He is the way, the truth, and the life. He's the gatekeeper—offering safety, security, and protection. You recognize his voice, submit to his call, and walk through the open gate—a recovery where addiction is replaced by freedom. No one comes to the Father except through the good shepherd.

Lord, thanks for honoring my feeble efforts to seek you. I'm grateful you came and found me when lost. Amen.

JEREMIAH 29:12-13; JOHN 10:7-14, 14:6

His Path Is the Way

Your daily discovery of Jesus' presence opens the door to discern his path for you. When you walk through it, the Spirit instructs you in the way you should go. The One who saved you will counsel and watch over you. In the present moment, your future is secure. It's essential when reaching a fork in the road, to submit to the Holy Spirit's guidance, rather than the enemy's map.

The enemy attempts to trick you to take the trail to the dry, arid, desert back to Egypt. God declares his fresh path of adventure is the only way. Faith in the creator, when tested, is fertilizer for your endurance to grow. He didn't save you to live a routine existence conforming to those around you.

The power of the presence of the Great I Am is in you so his love will flow through you. Your attitude begins to change when God loves another addict through you.

Lord, I praise you for the mighty men who remind me daily your presence in me is 24/7. Amen.

PSALM 32:8; JAMES 1:3; PHILIPPIANS 2:5

Rejoice in His Presence

While taking baby-steps to trust that only God knows what's best for you, your desire to check out his plan blossoms. As the sweetness of his presence lingers, and you begin the day with, "Good morning, Lord," the chaos and distraction in your busy mind lessen. Take a timely moment to strap on the full armor of God so you can stand against the devil's schemes. Love expels all fear.

Your daily encounter with Abba Father is overwhelming, and because you've fled to him for refuge, you can take hold of the hope that lies before you with confidence. God smiles and celebrates every time a ragged child reaches out to him.

Rest in his lap throughout the day, in spite of situations that overtake you. Know God will finish the work he has begun. How does this happen? Just stay out of his way!

God, I humbly ask for grace to check with you in the morning, afternoon, and evening. Abba Father, I love my time in your gentle, protective lap. Amen.

EPHESIANS 6:11; 1 JOHN 4:18; HEBREWS 6:18; PHILIPPIANS 1:6

Enemy-Trained

When admitting you are poor, needy, and totally powerless, you beg the Lord to hear your cry for mercy and deliver you from the depths of the grave. Confronting pointed fingers, your judgmental-self lingers. The moment you surrender to God's way, his love will stick and stay.

The devil's invitation to medicate with drugs, alcohol, gambling, and other addictions took you to some dreary and hopeless places. The enemy trained you in shame, guilt, pain, and death. In recovery, receive God's training of grace, mercy, and righteousness. Go for it. You've nothing to lose, yet everything to gain.

Upon accepting your poverty of spirit, you become grateful for your next breath, you appreciate recovery, and you're thankful for accountability. Don't settle for a normal, okay recovery. Go all in to have an amazing recovery and experience freedom.

Lord, I'm grateful you heard my cry for mercy. I'm tired of me. Give me grace to not settle for less than what you have for me. Amen.

Psalms 86:1, 13, 6:9

Thinking Highly of Yourself

Loosen up and be okay with only moving three feet on your journey today. The enemy suggests if you don't do twenty-five miles on the walk of perfection today, you've failed. God is excited about your progress and celebrates what you consider small gain as an overcoming victory. The one who saves is your great encourager and advocate. You've believed the destroyer during addiction; now it's your season to embrace the one who saved you.

God's Spirit whispers you're his beloved and strengthens you to break the bondage of regret. He leads you from the dark, gloomy forest of dead trees into a glorious, beautiful field of flowers. Your life depends on receiving his happiness. As God takes your burdens, you help others carry theirs.

Be on guard so you don't think you're better than anyone else; it's a devious enemy trick. Jesus was quite clear on this when he said whatever was done for the least deserving was done for him.

Lord, I pray for strength to not become weary of doing good. I'm grateful you're happy each time I plow through distractions to talk with you. Amen.

Psalm 86:4; Galatians 6:2,3,9; Matthew 25:40

Hope and Faith

As God's Spirit continues to connect you to himself, God reveals his extreme love by giving up his only Son. Why would he do that if he didn't have hope and faith in you? He loved you before you loved yourself. If you don't know God's love, you can't love anybody, much less yourself.

Jesus demonstrated his earth-shattering love by choosing to walk out his Father's plan. His perfect love is too great to fully understand. Whose life has benefitted from your life? God gave his Son; all he asks of you is to mix together your heart with a seed of child-like faith, along with knowing he's your only hope.

Why do you need to have a deeper understanding and expression of God's love for you? Because in deep recovery, you'll need a deeper capacity for his love to sustain your freedom.

Lord, I pray for courage to go forward on my knees, asking for faith to accept you accepting me. I desire to share your radical love with another person who is struggling with being loved. Amen.

JOHN 3:16, 15:13; ROMANS 5:8; EPHESIANS 3:18

Dismantle Your Scaffolding

You must love the Lord your God with all your heart, soul, and mind. You've sought love in all the wrong places attempting to medicate the pain, hide deep-seated issues, and fill the emptiness only God can fill. Addicts sabotage love, going out of the way to make themselves unlovable.

You're not only powerless over your addiction, you're also powerless over people, places, and things. Yet, you continue to think you have all the answers. Even when you're sober, you're still *you*! God's instruction is to be filled with love that comes from a pure heart, a clear conscience, and genuine faith. You need to plow up the hard ground of your heart to access the love that will save your life.

Scaffolding is a temporary structure, supporting workers who repair the exterior. When you get distracted, the inside work stops as you focus on what's happening outside. Get off the scaffolding; get back inside, and find the love you've been searching for.

Lord, I'm grateful you proclaim all who love your name will be filled with joy. I love your name. I ask you to dismantle my exterior scaffolding and have your Spirit work inside me. Amen.

MATTHEW 22:37; 1 TIMOTHY 1:5; HOSEA 10:12; PROVERBS 8:17; PSALM 5:11

His Quiet Whisper

During powerful prayer and devotion time, the enemy might begin to bang loudly on your door. God's giving you an opportunity to focus, increase your endurance, and grow in your faith. Remember, your recovery into freedom is a marathon, not a sprint. When your faith is tested, your endurance has a chance to grow.

Tests and trials are for you to stay where God has placed you—to run a bit longer without getting winded. When God's love breaks through, you hear his still, quiet whisper. Powerful winds blow you off course, earthquakes tear apart the ground around you, and a raging fire burns so close; yet, the Lord was not in any of those. After the wind, earthquake, and fire came a gentle whisper—God's voice.

Searching for God in only big places might cause you to miss your intimate moments with him—when his whisper comes in the quietness of a humbled heart.

Lord, I'm so grateful to leave my mess and climb into your lap to rest. I pray for grace to hear when you knock, and to open the door to welcome you in. Amen.

JAMES 1:3; 1 KINGS 19:11-12; REVELATION 3:20

Do Something

Your pride rebels when God begins doing something new, making a pathway through the wilderness and creating rivers in your dry wasteland of life. There's some ripping and tearing going on between your way and God's. It seems painful at times because it is! Your flesh demands to make decisions out of emotion, while God invites you to make decisions by wisdom.

You have to *stop* something in order to *do* something about it. Your way is the path back to the bondage of addiction. God's way is the pilgrim's path of recovery, where you say no to the enemy's lies and a glorious yes to the one who saved you.

With child-like faith, respond to Jesus' last words from the cross he climbed to save you. Yes, *it is finished*. You can do another day in recovery by God's grace.

Lord, I ask for grace to stop doing it my way. I ask for your strength to walk in what you have already finished for me. Amen.

ISAIAH 43:19; PHILIPPIANS 4:13; MATTHEW 5:37; JOHN 19:30

Character Issues

Addiction took you to dark places, possibly further than you ever wanted to go. Willpower, and thinking you had all the answers, never helped you get free from your addiction. Instead of shame and disgrace, God is faithful and ready to give you a double portion of blessing and everlasting joy.

Your recovery from addiction depends upon confronting the issues that were in you before medicating the pain—the why behind the what. This is an inside job, and you need to get out of his way for him to do his work in you.

Character issues will never sustain your new life in recovery; victim mentality and excessive misery must be confronted and removed before your heart hardens and takes you out. Deal with them, before they deal with you! What has to go? Everything that's connected with that old way of life. Trade insanity for sanity! If you look for God wholeheartedly, you will find him.

Lord, I praise you for ending my captivity, restoring me, and bringing me into recovery. Thanks so much for your patience. Amen.

Isaiah 61:7; Ephesians 4:22; Jeremiah 29:13-14

For the Foolish

Jesus' cross has long been a stumbling block to those the world considers wise. Only the inspired Word of God illuminates the path to the cross so that no one may boast. The apostle Paul didn't want to sound wise and persuasive; he wanted to be effective, and he was determined not to know anything except Jesus Christ crucified.

Your intellect and reasoning are roadblocks to faith and grace. When you were utterly powerless, Christ lifted you out from the dismal place you were in, and into recovery. His blood makes you right in his Father's sight. The intellectuals consider it irrational foolishness: that a man declared guilty and sentenced to crucifixion could be called King, Messiah, and Savior. The shipwrecked, ragged child embraces his kingdom by faith. It is because of what Jesus did that you're made right with the Father.

It's a dramatic turnaround; those world considers wise are absurd and foolhardy; those the world considers foolish have wisdom, peace, and understanding.

Lord, I am grateful for your shed blood on the cross, and that your priceless gift of eternal life was for someone as foolish as me. Amen.

1 CORINTHIANS 1:29, 2:2-4; ROMANS 5:6, 9; GALATIANS 3:24

Pursue Recovery

Make every effort to add to your faith, goodness, knowledge, self-control, perseverance, godliness, mutual affection, and love. These principles are the building blocks of a strong recovery, which will get you to the finish line. Seeking God first in all things will empower you to be tenacious in pursuing your recovery and a new life of purpose and blessings. Your past is forgiven, the present is fulfilling, and your future is secure. Trust God to guide and teach you in his truth.

The flesh demands instant gratification—I want what I want, now! God's work is not dependent on your work; it's working constantly in your life. This is progress, not perfection. Don't listen to the enemy's lies that say God didn't hear you and you're not doing enough.

When you desire Jesus' presence, he helps you return to him on a daily basis and instructs you how to wait on him. The waiting seems a bit easier when you rest in Jesus' lap, because time with the Son of God transforms a busy, hectic day into a day of serenity.

Lord, I need your grace to finish the race. I'm grateful you're working on my behalf, even when I think you're taking too long. Amen.

2 PETER 1:5-7; PSALMS 25:5, 37:7; HOSEA 12:6

A Blessing

Your addiction was a blessing because despair and brokenness got you to the place that God was all you had left. He answered your prayer, saved you, and set you into recovery to begin anew. No longer about you, it's now all about him. You stop being a taker, and begin to be a giver. The condition of your heart determines the course of your life, and your only protection is to operate in God's grace and tender mercies.

Before all else, give your heart to the one who knows your heart. Addiction hardened your heart with no hope. You no longer need to dangle your toes off the edge of the cliff to the dark abyss. Be encouraged on your imperfect journey, and don't beat yourself up when falling short. Abba Father delights in each step you take toward him.

Lord, I'm grateful your love kept me safe when standing at the edge of the cliff. Guard my heart so my blessing can become a blessing to others. Amen.

PROVERBS 4:23; 2 CORINTHIANS 9:7; JEREMIAH 17:9

One Foot out the Door

In your feeble humanness, you're either doing the deal in recovery, or you're watching from the sidelines with one foot out the door. There's no middle ground; you're going forward or slipping back.

You start recovery as a young child wearing diapers and drinking from a sippy-cup. Soon, the enemy snares you with one of his favorite tricks—his gospel of busyness. Busyness distracts you from seeking God first. Soon, you're missing meetings and not being accountable to someone.

The fruits of busyness are exhaustion, distraction, and double-mindedness. It weakens you to the point of medicating because the Holy Spirit can no longer be heard. Then off you go again, speeding down the road of intellect to figure out, in your own power, how self-pity, judgment, resentment, and entitlement can be justified. God shows mercy to anyone he chooses, and whoever believes in him shall not be disappointed.

Lord, I desire to stumble into humility to admit my need for you sooner. I'm raising the white flag of surrender. I give my busyness to you. Amen.

1 TIMOTHY 6:6; ROMANS 9:15, 33

Stubbing Your Toe

God laid a stone that causes men to stumble and a rock that makes them fall. The rock you've tripped on is Jesus. You stumbled over him while believing the lies of the enemy, giving in to the demands of the flesh, choosing chaos, medicating your pain, and accepting curses. The best thing you've ever done is stubbing your toe on the rock, because you stumbled right into Jesus' lap.

Recovery gives you the opportunity to turn your will and life over to the creator. You've stumbled into becoming obedient to follow his path to recovery. Your stumbling in the past robbed and destroyed everything and almost killed you. God is now making you into one of his rocks on which he will build his church to receive another suffering addict.

Lord, I'm so grateful I stumbled over you. I praise you for the grace to stumble into you time and time again. Amen.

ROMANS 9:33; MATTHEW 16:18

Season to Recover

There is a season for everything, and it's your season for recovery. Allow the Word to be planted in your life, and allow God to water, fertilize, and be in charge of the harvest. Your recovery is lifeless without living water to nourish and empower you. Jesus invites you to come to him and drink! Old beliefs and laziness are weeds that restrict the very grace and mercy which fertilize your growth. The prison chain-gang of relapse constantly awaits.

Seek God, as a garden parched by the hot sun, and dare to trust your thirst can only be met by the Son of God. When you discover who he is, and what he will do for you, you'll ask for his nourishment.

This is your season to embrace or let go, turn into or away, listen or speak, keep going or give up, and receive living water or stay in the desert. God declares you're worthy to experience the harvest, and he promises you will at the proper time if you don't give up.

Lord, I pray for grace to be thirsty for your living Word and courage to drink of it. I'm so tired of the chain-gang. Amen.

Ecclesiastes 3:1; John 4:10, 7:37; Galatians 6:9

His Truth Is Freedom

As you check out what recovery looks like, a sense of overwhelming gratitude grows because you know God saved you from certain destruction. It's a challenge to think you're worthy of God's unending grace and tender mercies, and that's okay because you aren't! God's the one who made you worthy to become the person he says you are: to discover his plans and purpose for you.

Read and study his Word, which is living and active, and allow it to expose, sift, analyze, and judge the thoughts and attitudes of your heart. Since the beginning, the Word was with God, and the Word was God himself.

The Father, by his Word, begins to separate you for himself. The truth, which sets you free, is his bag of seeds to fulfill your needs. God has been very patient with you because he desires you to be his, set apart and re-positioned into his next dimension.

Lord, I desire to study your Word: the truth that sets me free.
It's amazing you made me worthy to become free. Amen.

HEBREWS 4:12; JOHN 17:17; JOHN 1:1

The Word Never Changes

God's Word will never pass away; it doesn't change or adapt to your circumstance. The truth is, without God, there's no victory over any challenge. Do you dare trust that he can handle any situation that threatens to hurt, punish, or destroy you. It's essential for your recovery to get off the crazy, insane, demented roller-coaster of emotions which make your decisions. God's Word is the ultimate authority. The grass withers, the flower fades, but the Word of God stands forever.

If you don't believe in something, you'll fall for anything. God's revelation is the opportunity to believe in something everlasting, eternal, and never-changing. You will know with clarity that God's the ultimate authority of all things and the one who existed before creation.

The God-breathed Word is useful to inspire, teach, rebuke, correct, train you in righteousness, and thoroughly equip you for every good work. Check out recovery; your eternal life depends on it.

Lord, I don't have a clue where to go or what to do, and I am grateful your Word is a lamp to my feet and a light to my path. Amen.

MATTHEW 24:35; ISAIAH 40:8; 2 TIMOTHY 3:16-17; PSALM 119:105

Confidence in His Word

Will you discover God's path without study of the Word or having respect for his ways? Absolutely not! He lights your path, marks it, and gives the grace to walk on it. He gives you strength to endure, tender mercies to continue, and showers blessings along the way. He guards the course of the just and protects the way of his faithful ones, while preparing a mansion upon reaching your eternal destination. The trip can get rough at times, so stay focused on your destination.

Abba Father already knows what his path for you looks like. He guides you into the future, declares your identity, and reveals his will for you. He created you to choose him; in fact, he chose you before the foundation of the world, even while you were in the throes of addiction.

If your faith isn't in the Word, you're on the wrong path. Faith in his Word gives you the ability to walk the path into your recovery.

Lord, I'm so grateful it's what I know in your Word that's going to keep me. I have confidence you're taking care of all this stuff. Amen.

PSALM 119:15; PROVERBS 2:8; GALATIANS 1:4

Reflection of His Word

The Word ignites your very purpose and always produces fruit. It will accomplish all God wants it to and prosper everywhere he sends it. With the mind of a child, you can believe that regardless of what you were, where you've come, or what you're planning this very moment—he chose you, and his Word will set you free. Stay out of that craziness between your ears—you can't comprehend or figure this out; you have to experience it.

How near and dear has the Bible been for you? It's okay if there's dust on the front cover. There's no shame; just encouragement to read about who he is and what he will do for you. Then the Word is near you: on your lips and in your heart.

The key is the practical application of God's Word in your life, as you become grafted into him. The enemy will do all in his power to keep the Word on the shelf and off your lips because it's with the mouth that you confess and are saved.

Lord, I desire to get closer to you through your Word. Help me show by my actions that I live in the truth. Amen.

Isaiah 55:11; Romans 10:8, 10

Confidence in God

You can't fight the dark forces and the spirit of heaviness with weapons of this world. One weapon with divine power to demolish strongholds is to put on the garment of praise. At an early age, seeds of destruction were planted in your garden to harden your heart, steal your identity, and destroy your blessings.

Jesus declared the enemy was a murderer and the father of lies from the beginning. Condemnation is an attack upon confidence, but it's more of a heart issue. Even if your heart condemns you, God is greater than your heart.

The only way you know if you belong to the truth is by your actions—believing in the name of Jesus and loving one another as he commanded. God's love is difficult to comprehend. His love lives in you by the Spirit he gave you.

Lord, thanks for the confidence in knowing you forgave me, which released me. I'm tired of tying myself up in knots of condemnation. Amen.

2 CORINTHIANS 10:4; JOHN 8:44; 1 JOHN 3:20-24

Enemy Strongholds

A stronghold is present when the same negative thought keeps rearing its ugly head. The enemy will use what's worked against you to keep you in slavery. The liar's goal is to get you to hate yourself. Thoughts like *I must be bad, look at all the bad things I've done* or *I have no hope* plague you. Fear assaults trust and rest; addiction affects areas of love; rejection comes as unworthiness; confusion attacks decision making; and witchcraft feeds power and control.

You don't have to fight alone. God's divine power smashes strongholds, and provides the sufficient grace to withstand any enemy attack. The truth is you're an adopted child of the Most High God. When you desire to do what's right, and end up doing the very thing you hate, you wonder who will free you from addiction. The answer is Jesus Christ.

Lord, thanks for taking my cares and sustaining me. I ask for your courage to trust you more fully and deeply. Amen.

ZECHARIAH 4:6; ROMANS 7:15, 24-25; PSALM 55:22

Conform?

Conforming to this world has never worked out. You've been tricked, beaten, and bruised with your flesh making the decisions, as the sinful nature's always hostile to God. The enemy hoodwinked you that your needs would be met by searching for love in all the wrong places.

Moments of clarity gave momentary hope, but the discipline needed to change was lacking. The Lord knows you tried. Your recovery is greatly threatened by conforming to what other people think, or having external circumstances ruin your day.

Your first response to hurt may have always been to react with anger. The selfish, arrogant, stubborn flesh isn't going away without a struggle. You're still dealing with consequences from medicating your pain, shame, and guilt. God's pleasing, and perfect will for your life is that His Spirit controls your mind, and you find peace and life.

Lord, I ask you to fix my thoughts on what is true, honorable, right, pure, lovely, and admirable. Amen.

ROMANS 8:6, 7, 12:2; ACTS 20:35; PHILIPPIANS 4:8

Start Fresh

In recovery, the levels and dimensions experienced on a daily basis can fluctuate. There will be growth and maturity in some areas, while in other areas you're still a babe in diapers. Everyone who believes that Jesus is the Christ has become a child of God—not a teenager, young adult, or older person— you're simply one of his kids. You start fresh and new, climb into Jesus' lap, and take your sippy cup with you.

Set aside past experiences with religion or church, forgive the godly people who betrayed and hurt you, and let go of the religious Pharisees who condemned you in the name of the Bible. Religion is for those who are afraid to go to hell; spirituality is for those who have experienced it on earth.

Lay past resentments at the foot of the cross, and receive the Father's tender love with the faith of a small child. Start over. Know God forgives you, Jesus' blood cleanses you, and the Holy Spirit empowers you.

Lord, I wanted a double-burger with extra onions; yet, today, I know I need milk, not solid food. Amen.

1 JOHN 5:1; MATTHEW 10:14; HEBREWS 5:12

You Can Do All Things

It's okay when you're at the end of the rope and one step forward seems impossible, because when you're done, God's strength begins. When God throws you a lifeline, your stubborn flesh demands a pity party to keep rehearsing past hurts and resentments. If you don't hang on to the lifeline, you're soon off recovery's path and you'll crash for the umpteenth time.

God gives you strength to do everything through him: to look ahead, not behind. Jesus is able to save those who come to the Father through him. His breath of life will deliver, refresh, and reassure you. He intercedes for you, and through him you have access to the Father by the Holy Spirit.

Your situation might not change, yet the Holy Spirit empowers you to deal with it before it deals with you. This is about progress, not perfection. As you embrace the Holy Spirit's fire ignited within, accept yourself as you truly are: a ragged child, poor in spirit. You can do all things through God, and enjoy one more day free of addiction.

Lord, thanks for knowing me and setting me apart before I was born. I praise you for being so patient with me. Amen.

PHILIPPIANS 4:13; HEBREWS 2:18, 7:25; JEREMIAH 1:5

Poison Arrows

Past remembrances of pain, guilt, and shame pop up in a flash. The evil one shoots his fiery arrows, which stick, and if not dealt with, the toxicity of the poison places your recovery at great risk. Your shield of faith allows you to identify enemy attacks. When you dare trust the Lord with all your heart, and acknowledge him in all your ways, the enemy's flaming darts can't stick. Because you're human, sometimes one will stick for a bit and go unnoticed. Then you need people to help identify it so you can ask God to remove it.

With child-like faith, you believe God will intervene and remove anything you give him. For you know that when your faith is tested, your endurance has a chance to grow. God's truth and light are more than you ever hoped for, beyond what you ever prayed for. They exceed your wildest dreams.

The Holy Spirit's fire within gives the courage to start walking toward what God has for you. When he reveals to you what he's prepared, it will blow your mind!

Lord, I'm thankful every knee must bow before you, including mine. I desire your shield to deflect enemy arrows, your Word as my sword, and your cross for deliverance. Amen.

EPHESIANS 6:16; PSALM 3:5-6; JAMES 1:3; 1 CORINTHIANS 2:9-10

When the Furnace Gets Hot

You're made to do more than just survive, and God teaches you to remain standing firm on his foundation by refining you in the furnace of suffering. This is a challenge to all who want God's good stuff while sitting in a recliner with their feet up.

You discover what you're capable of when persevering and embracing problems and trials on a daily basis. Instead of a hissy-fit when the furnace heat gets turned up, you can rejoice because you know it's okay.

The enemy always takes you further than you want to go. It's during these trials you know the Lord is with you. He's right beside you when it gets hot. The purpose of God's instruction is that you be filled with love that comes from a pure heart, a clear conscience, and genuine faith. Without his refining, your faith life would be as a fig tree with no fruit. God needs your fruit so you are fit for his service—to help other addicts recover.

Lord, in the furnace my impurities are brought to light. Thanks for refining me for your purpose. Amen.

ISAIAH 48:10; ROMANS 5:3; PSALM 16:8; 1 TIMOTHY 1:5

Yoke of Offense

It is for freedom that Christ has set you free. God gives you the desire to do what's right; yet, your flesh entices you to do what you hate to do. A key strategy the devil often uses is to twist you into tiny knots by making you get offended by something or somebody. You're extremely sensitive, feel inadequate, and are irritated with yourself. Offense is all around you, and it invites you to participate. Stand firm in your recovery.

Your struggle is not against flesh and blood, but against the powers of this dark world and against the spiritual forces of evil in the heavenly realms. That's why you can get offended when the church service or Bible study is taking longer than you think it should. The enemy also works diligently to get you offended at the people close to you—to separate you from them.

The struggle is against the spirit of offense who's out to steal relationships and distract you from being in the present moment. Say no today to that strategy.

Lord, I desire to stand firm when feeling offended by words said, and not said; by actions done, or not done. Amen.

GALATIANS 5:1; ROMANS 7:15; EPHESIANS 6:12

Become Less

You need to check on how you're accepting others whose faith is weak, without judging or being offended by them. Many times your argument is not with people; you're arguing with yourself and it overflows onto others. The blessing is to be around survivors of the depths of hopelessness. As you embrace those God brings to you, you begin to embrace yourself. Expectations become less!

John the Baptist was in prison, wasting away. Alone in a dark dungeon, he may have been offended because Jesus seemed to be too busy to rescue him. He might have even doubted his divine assignment for his life. Instead, John remembered his own words: "I must become less, so he can become greater."

When God gives you an assignment, he's responsible for it. Your task is to become less, so he becomes greater. Stay faithful to your godly assignment to the end.

Lord, reveal any offensive way in me, and lead me in the way everlasting. I desire to complete your assignment. Amen.

ROMANS 14:1; MATTHEW 11:6,4; JOHN 3:30; PSALM 139:24

The Old Man Has to Go

You're not defined by what others say. They're talking about "the old you" who used to make decisions based on feelings and emotions. Many have a difficult time separating themselves from their old self. After setting down the addiction, the real work starts with changing your mind—how and why you think certain things. God invites you to allow him to transform you into a new person by changing the way you think. He can renew your mind.

Addiction bit you powerfully enough to die, yet you survived. This illustrates that God's calling on your life is stronger than anything you've endured or experienced. Everything you went through was God's purpose to get you into recovery. You've been through hell, but you're still standing, and the past no longer controls your future.

Your old self has to go! Jesus died to make you worthy, his blood cleansed you, and when walking the last mile to your brutal execution, he called the warden to give you a full pardon.

Lord, I'm grateful you are setting my mind on things above. Thanks for letting me see myself as you see me: a brand new person in Christ. Amen.

ROMANS 12:2; EPHESIANS 4:22-24; COLOSSIANS 3:2

Become a Fool to Become Wise

Forget everything except Jesus Christ—the one who was crucified. Come to him in your weakness: timid and trembling. Choose not to go into the battlefield of your mind for clever thoughts, reasons, or excuses. It's only in the power of the Holy Spirit, who gives revelation, that you're still out of prison and above ground.

Your reasoning and intellect cannot explain spiritual truths, for the wisdom of this world is foolishness to God. Pride absolutely hates the idea you have to become a fool to become wise by God's standards.

Your flesh demands to be in control, while the enemy comes to steal what God has for you. Thank God you have an advocate who testifies the truth. Jesus forgives your sins, wipes your slate clean, and remembers your sins and lawless acts no more. The enemy invites you to muddle in the past shame and guilt, and become anxious about your future. The Holy Spirit whispers, "My beloved, take my hand, and walk into your recovery with me. I am well pleased with your efforts." Who will you listen to today?

Lord, I desire to become a fool to become wise by your standards. This day, I want to take your hand and walk with you. Amen.

1 CORINTHIANS 2:2-4, 10, 3:18-19; HEBREWS 10:17

You're Not a Mistake

Guilt makes you feel you've *made* a mistake, while shame makes you feel you *are* a mistake. The enemy digs guilt and shame out of his bag of strategies to entice you to believe there's no forgiveness. The enemy tricks you into thinking you're a bad person, that you're unworthy of any good thing. The enemy's always trying to take from you, while God's always ready to give.

The lies of the enemy are totally dismantled and erased as the Holy Spirit leads you into all truth. You know him, and he lives in you. You're one of the world's great sabotage experts in self-destruction. Brokenness comes when you recognize you did everything to yourself. When you repent and confess to God, he forgives, and reveals that your shame and guilt were nailed to Jesus' cross. Knowing this truth is what sets you free.

It's essential to check on your spiritual condition and have people who encourage you to keep moving forward. God's Spirit helps you when you're weak and intercedes on your behalf for any circumstance before you.

Lord, thanks for your forgiveness. You say you will remember my sins no more. I'm grateful to know your truth. Help me not to listen to the enemy's lies. Amen.

JOHN 8:32, 14:17; ROMANS 8:26; HEBREWS 8:12

Your Time

No matter how wrong things seem to be, everything is okay with God and his world. The simplicity of your recovery begins to seep into your mind and heart when you get your inside world put right. This allows you to see God in the everyday, outside world around you. When confusion, chaos, worry, and fear rise from the pit of hell, you resist and stand firm in the faith because all in recovery are going through the same kind of suffering. Your victim mentality is being replaced with a victor mindset.

Once lost, God adopted you into his family: guilty, now forgiven; in darkness, now in the light of the Son of God; dead in sin, now spiritually alive. When you fall, get back up; when a storm hits, endure; when he speaks, listen. Fight against giving up, and hang in there until your head hits the pillow tonight.

This is your season to recover. You haven't lost time, and no longer have to wonder how it got so late so soon. When you get your inside world put right, there's sufficient time for everything needed to get done.

Lord, thanks for child-like faith and the truth that my life's last years will be the best. Amen.

MATTHEW 5:8; 1 PETER 5:9; ECCLESIASTES 3:1

Stay One More Day

Everyone on this planet is in recovery from something. As you mature in accepting powerlessness as a gift, it's a daily reprieve based on your willingness and obedience. It's great comfort to learn the war you've struggled with all these years was decided, once and for all, at Jesus' cross.

You can access his power and resources to live the abundant life you're worthy to experience. This is an inside job. As water reflects the face, so life reflects the heart. Impossible? Nothing will be impossible for you, through him! Your tiniest faith can move mountains that block the path, and kill the giants waiting to ambush you along the way. You're showing great faith to stay clean another day, trusting in the Lord.

God responds when you admit to being poor in spirit. He is always near those who have a broken heart. This is serious business: stay, recover, and live in freedom, or run, relapse, and live in bondage.

Lord, thanks for your grace and desire to stay one more day. I pray my life will reflect the great work you're doing on my heart. Amen.

PROVERBS 27:19; MATTHEW 17:20; PSALMS 31:14, 34:18

Shepherds Are a Gift

Your best thinking got you into police cars, waiting on the corner in driving rain, living in a car at a casino parking lot, drinking in secret, stealing pain meds, and hiding in a closet when the doorbell rang. In recovery, you need spiritual shepherds who will feed you with knowledge and understanding, help, guide, and hold you accountable on a daily basis.

The followers of Jesus were ordinary human beings who were taught by the Son of God to carry his message of salvation. Yet, they only became effective after the Holy Spirit descended upon them. The fruit of the Holy Spirit are evident in those empowered by the Spirit.

Tag along with your shepherds and mirror their actions. The fruit of the righteous is a tree of life, providing shade from the intense heat of the enemy's lies. When refreshed by shepherds, you learn to refresh others. Embrace your shepherds: they're a priceless gift to help save your life.

Lord, thanks for the shade of your tree of life. Bless the shepherds you've given me, to train me by their example. Amen.

JEREMIAH 3:15; PROVERBS 11:25, 30

Saved from Yourself

God places his seal of ownership on you. He has a plan and purpose for your life, and empowers you to live a sober life by putting his Spirit in your heart as a deposit. God's deposit of himself into you, without reservation, begins to transform your mind.

The radical truth is God keeps no memory of your past sins; condemnation is from the pit of hell. Quit beating yourself up, and climb into Jesus' lap to rest in him. Invite the Spirit to speak through you to others still suffering.

God's seal of ownership will keep you sober and clean one day at a time. The Holy Spirit convicts you of the need to be saved from yourself, and warns you when small compromises sneak in. Many relapses happen when you're feeling comfortable. Be on guard when you're doing well. The enemy hits you with entitlement and his reward system based on a lie: a little celebration wouldn't hurt! It's never a great crash in one day; it's always a slow fade. There's no middle ground. You're either pursuing recovery or falling back into relapse.

Lord, thanks for setting your seal on me and your Spirit in me. I had no clue you would gift me with so much more of yourself. Amen.

2 CORINTHIANS 1:22; HEBREWS 10:17; MATTHEW 10:20; JOHN 16:8

Benefits and Gifts

God's seal of ownership guarantees you belong to him, and releases benefits with an eternal bonus. His deposit of himself totally, unequivocally, and without reservation declares throughout the universe that salvation is now yours. The benefits include a new mind and heart, no memory of your sins, an advocate, a teacher, a reminder, peace, and being set apart for his use. God also gifts you with great faith, knowledge, and discernment. Are these gifts producing fruit in your life?

Faith allows you to walk on his path of recovery one day at a time. It gives you knowledge to know what the next right thing to do is, and discernment to identify the enemy's tricks and the rebellion of the flesh.

When feeling a bit stretched beyond anything you've ever experienced, that's okay—you're in new territory. Your addiction was physically, emotionally, and spiritually killing you. Resentments, however petty they seemed, kept you locked and loaded to medicate. Gratitude for recovery beats down control issues and helps you keep pursuing your new life of benefits and gifts.

Lord, thanks for deeming me worthy for your seal of ownership. I'm grateful for your greatest gift—your Son. I had no clue your benefits and other gifts were so amazing. Amen.

2 CORINTHIANS 1:22; HEBREWS 10:15-17; JOHN 14:26-27

Consider Trials Joy

Your invitation to rejoice when running into problems and trials is the most radical, revolutionary proposition ever considered. Doing it your way to reason and manipulate your way out of situations always had less than desirable results. The enemy always won the battle going on between your ears, as intellectual dissection is a dead-end with frustration and blame.

You're to consider it joy when you face problems. Everything has a purpose. Problems and trials teach you to endure for the blessing on the other side. Endurance is about surviving regardless of what you think or feel. As you persevere in exercising your faith, fear, distrust, and anger are slowly replaced by love, trust, and calmness.

Give the same effort for your recovery as you did your addiction. God lifted you from the muck and chose you to become a warrior on the battlefield. Abba Father strengthens you to trust him with any problems and trials. Rest in him.

Lord, thanks for your patience with me when problems show up. I'm so grateful when attempting to figure it out, you whisper, "trust me" in my ear. Amen.

ROMANS 5:3; JAMES 1:2; 2 PETER 1:5

Accept His Gift

It's for freedom that Christ has set you free. The Father's unrelenting love protected you while lost, until you could finally admit you were at the end of your rope. In fact, you were hanging onto the last knot, ready to give up, when God's hand lifted you from that life-threatening situation.

Remember the urgency of your emergency because it awaits you if burdened once again by the slavery of addiction. You begin recovery as a new babe in diapers and must be a bit patient and tender with yourself. This is a marathon of endurance, not a sprint to instant gratification.

Each new step into sobriety builds confidence that God set you on the rock, a foundation, so you don't fall for anything. By his gift of faith, you eagerly await for a new day. Jesus delivered his package of wholeness to your doorstep. You have the choice to accept his gift and open it, and receive His power to begin your healing.

Lord, thanks that your hope will be an anchor for my soul. I'm grateful you won't let go of me, never, ever. Amen.

GALATIANS 5:1, 5; HEBREWS 6:19

Fruit of Your Lips

The old has gone and the new has come. God is making you into an extraordinary new creation, while renewing you day by day. When introducing yourself as an addict, you're speaking of who you used to be. God says you're no longer that person.

You were sick and tired with no place to go. God answered your cry by sending his Spirit with a sledge hammer to begin his demolition project, and rebuild you—stone by stone. His Word renovates, and the truth sets you free.

You barely survived to get into recovery, and it's essential to speak words of life. You now open your lips to speak what is right, and share wisdom. God says you're a champion: he blesses you with grace, and declares you're worthy. What comes from your lips protects you and honors God. Your sacrifice of praise is the fruit of lips that confess his name. This is heavy-duty combat, spiritual warfare. Jesus invites you to confess his name, and speak his living Word over yourself and others, so you don't stumble over words that speak death.

Lord, help me stay out of your dumpster, trying to take back stuff you've thrown. I desire to confess your name with my lips. Amen.

2 CORINTHIANS 5:17; JOHN 8:32; PROVERBS 8:6; HEBREWS 13:15

A Tender and Responsive Heart

From your heart spring the issues of life, which led you to medicate your pain in the deep, dark valley of addiction. God rewards us for our conduct, according to what our deeds deserve.

The heart is deceitful; pain, unforgiveness, and resentment are stored there. By his grace, you no longer make poor choices while in chaos and confusion. You begin by admitting your bad relationships had something to do with you. If you can't admit the damage caused while using, you'll continue to create havoc, injure, and hurt others while in recovery.

This isn't about putting the plug in the jug, setting the drug down, or staying out of the casino: this is about living in freedom. By God's grace, you no longer allow your heart to make decisions. The Father replaces your stony, stubborn heart with a tender, responsive one, and his Spirit helps you make your decisions with wisdom and the truth.

Lord, I desire a more tender and responsive heart. I'm excited for your care after surgery. Amen.

PROVERBS 4:23; JEREMIAH 17:9-10; EZEKIEL 36:26

Saved to Save Another

When your old deceitful heart was replaced by the Father's tender and loving heart, Jesus' blood began flowing through every vein and artery. His Spirit nudges you to tell others about his marvelous works. You can't keep it unless you give it away.

Your new heart's desire to do it God's way overrides your way. The always-present danger is losing your sense of urgency. Decisions made without counsel or advice are red flags—a set-up to sabotage your recovery.

God's already begun to do something new in your life, making a way in the desert and creating rivers in the wasteland of your past. God answered your cry to lift you out of the place you were, and set you on solid ground. Each new day is a great day, regardless of what happens. Your assignment for this day is to get to the next right place, and do the next right thing.

Lord, I desire to tell others of your marvelous works. I pray I will have a great day, even if bad things happen. Amen.

PSALM 9:1; ISAIAH 43:19

Pilate's Courtyard

Summing up all that's taught in God's law, you should do for others what you would like them to do for you. The enemy tricked you into doing to others, before they did it to you. Regret and shame from the past fuel self-condemnation. In a twisted, dark dance of deflection from self, you medicated your pain with your addiction.

While in Pilate's courtyard yelling, "Crucify him," you're shocked to look up at the man and discover it's you, not Jesus! Abba Father steps in to declare there's hope in his unfailing love. Tap into his loving lifeline. You don't need to be crucified because Jesus already sacrificed himself for you.

You are urged, in view of God's mercy, to offer yourself as a pleasing sacrifice to him. You are transformed with a renewed mind. You now become the golden rule.

Lord, I'm grateful to be a living sacrifice, not a dead one. Thanks for replacing my self-destruction with your transforming construction. Amen.

MATTHEW 7:12; PSALM 130:7; ROMANS 12:1

The Same Effort

Don't get tired of doing what's good, and don't get discouraged to the point of giving up. Don't agree with the enemy's lies: *I'm tired. I don't have time.* Exhaustion comes when operating in your own strength. Trust in Jesus' strength to be effective and productive. Submit, get out of his way, and become obedient as his Spirit activates his truth in you.

Remember, it's progress not perfection. Missing meetings, lacking a mentor, having a victim mentality, holding on to resentment, and the entitlement mindset keep you ineffective and unproductive. Check yourself: is your recovery getting as much time and effort as your addiction once did?

You're on a recovery crusade to glorify God, who saved you, and he provides the courage to go all in and get as serious in recovery as you were in addiction.

Lord, thanks for your strength to do what's good and not give up. I desire to give you the effort I gave my addiction. Amen.

GALATIANS 6:9; 2 PETER 1:8

A Parent's Word

At the Last Supper, Jesus knew he was going to return to his Father. He showed the disciples the full extent of his love. The Father had given him authority over everything and what did he do? He washed the disciple's feet—even the one who he knew would betray him. He set an example of how we should love others.

As a child, you couldn't separate what your parents said from who they were. Your tiny brain couldn't understand the words spoken over you, and possibly interpreted them differently than intended, perhaps even causing emotional detachment.

Only the heavenly Father's words can set you free from your earthly parents' words. Jesus revealed his Father's love through the cross. He came to restore you to your heavenly Father, so you can identify and let go of issues concerning your earthly parents with love.

Father, I'm grateful my parents did the very best they could. Jesus, thanks for giving yourself to your Father, so we can also give ourselves to him. Amen.

JOHN 13:1, 3, 15, 17, 34; JOHN 17:9

Purposed to Recover

Your addict behavior was fighting an imaginary opponent and running a marathon with no finish line. With child-like faith and baby steps, you begin walking with purpose in each step of your recovery.

The enemy of your soul is out to compromise your recovery by using all your strength shadowboxing. One wrong step can quickly cancel out the many steps already taken, so you purpose to please God, not people. Transfer your expertise in people-pleasing to pleasing the one who examines your heart. God will honor your desire to please him.

Without purpose, your recovery's in danger of complacency and laziness. Pride creeps in and soon you're no longer teachable, lacking discipline to do the next right thing. God brings people to stand with you in one spirit and one purpose who accept you as you truly are with no drama. Be watchful for those who will teach you wisdom and discipline, and welcome them with open arms. They will be your guides to assist you to discover your purpose. You're no longer alone.

Lord, I desire to please you, not people. Thanks for my purpose: to love others still suffering in addiction. Amen.

1 CORINTHIANS 9:26; 1 THESSALONIANS 2:4; PHILIPPIANS 1:27; PROVERBS 1:2

Healing in Confession

God's Spirit guides you to confront the false self in order to become who you truly are—the beloved of Jesus. With reckless abandon, acknowledge your emptiness and step over the stumbling blocks of manipulation and control that will, absolutely, sabotage your recovery.

Healing begins when you confess your sins to others and become accountable to a power greater than yourself. God reminds you to not be fearful because he's always with you, and will strengthen, help, and uphold you. A little more work? No, a little more faith!

In recovery, you dare to let go and pray: "O God, have mercy on me, according to your loving kindness; by your tender mercies, blot out my transgressions." God takes your shame and guilt as far as the east is from the west; Jesus forgives; and the Holy Spirit removes. As you become more authentic, the seed of honesty takes root so you know the Shepherd's way. If you desire people to be honest and open, start being an honest and open person. The blessing is you start believing who God says you are.

Lord, thanks for taking my past and filling all my new empty spots with your Truth, which sets me free. Amen.

JAMES 5:16; ISAIAH 41:10; PSALM 51:1

Emotions as a First Response

Suffering brought by lies is a type of torment that wounds deeply. God says he knows the slander of those opposing you. Instead of an emotional response to those who attack and belittle you, take the high road. Stay focused and be determined to walk through the emotions. Allow God to calm the storm and remember that his Word never changes.

Tough situations allow you to test your faith. Be reminded that God will sustain you through all of it. You didn't come into recovery on a winning streak, or have a good track record of taking care of your basic needs.

Don't let your emotions be your first response, no matter what people say. Remain focused and seek God first. Know you're right where God wants you to be. When opposition comes, trust God. Then you won't mismanage your circumstances.

Lord, I'm tired of letting my emotions make my decisions. I need your grace to stand on what you say. Thanks that your Word never changes. Amen.

REVELATION 2:9; 2 CORINTHIANS 13:5; 1 CORINTHIANS 16:18

Who's Your Leader?

Are you frustrated and unfulfilled, or a reflection of God's grace with joy? Jesus invites you to follow him. You no longer have to be tricked into doing the same things over and over, expecting different results. The spotlight is on God, not you. If you want to stand out, you have to step down and be a servant—simply be a mirror of God's grace.

Follow God or keep following yourself, embrace truth or believe lies, be encouraged or discouraged—these are choices that will lead you to recovery or relapse. It's also a choice to make no choice.

God's Spirit lives in you. You're now one of his kids drinking his living water. The devil constantly reminds you of being unworthy and unqualified, advertising that his poison has all the answers. As you choose God to lead you into your destiny of recovery and freedom, his truth will guide you to fight for your new life.

Lord, I'm grateful your Word is a lamp and a light to follow. Save me from following myself. Amen.

ACTS 20:24; LUKE 9:23; MATTHEW 23:11; 1 CORINTHIANS 6:19; JOHN 16:13

Apply God's Word

The Lord desires to direct your heart into God's love. With child-like faith, fix your thoughts on what is true, honorable, and right. Only then can you know what the Father has done for you. As gratitude begins to sprout within, you desire to do something for him. When you embrace his unconditional love, your once stony heart begins to soften. It becomes tender and responsive.

Your criticism of self and others lessens as you begin to experience a new life in recovery: a life of abundance through Jesus. The Spirit activates the living Word in you. Without his Spirit, your blinders remain.

When you study God's Word, you learn how to practically apply it. The words he speaks to you are spirit and life. This is all about God: human effort accomplishes nothing. Your new heart, submitted to God, allows his love to shine through you to others.

Lord, I had no idea how stubborn my heart was. I pray to remain faithful to studying your Word, so I can apply it to my everyday life. Amen.

2 THESSALONIANS 3:5; PHILIPPIANS 4:8; EZEKIEL 36:26; JOHN 6:63

Jesus Weeps with You

When Scripture tells us that Jesus wept, it reveals the profound emotion he had for his friend. He was deeply moved in spirit and troubled as he witnessed others weeping.

We've all faced sorrow in our lives: death of loved ones, loss of relationship, or rejection by those close to us. Sometimes it's the torture of regret, dreams and visions stolen, or self-inflicted pain. Jesus meets us right where we are. He knows our pain. When he sees us weeping, he weeps with us.

The One who weeps with you also offers a sanctuary of rest during distress. The Lord of emotions, humble and gentle, will teach you. Jesus is the example of humility, and his nourishment came from doing the will of the Father. By his example, you can admit you're in dire need of getting into the Lord's lap. He will weep with you, hug you, love you, and give you rest.

Lord, I'm so grateful you spoke life into my being. Thanks for weeping with me when I'm hurt. Amen.

JOHN 4:34, 11:33-35; MATTHEW 11:28-29

You Have an Enemy

Coaches and players study game film to devise plans and strategies against opponents. The player's practice, over and over, to prepare for the game. In school, you studied material to pass a test. Devise a plan and strategy to defeat the enemy. Practice daily for two weeks to read a devotional, call your accountability partner, read a Proverb, and make it to your meetings. It's a simple plan and strategy, yet there will be opposition.

God chose you before the foundation of the world, and when you choose him, the spiritual warfare intensifies. The war is not against other people, it's against spiritual forces of wickedness, and the battle rages between your ears. The devil, the father of lies, knows what you like and don't like, and he seeks to defeat you with a strategy of deceit.

The enemy's been messing with you since you were young. God's truth is the only way to be set free. You need constant reminders of his promises to remain standing firm in recovery.

Lord, I'm grateful for your weapons to fight the enemy of my soul—the Word, praise, and prayer. Thank you that the war has already been won at the cross, with the shed blood of your Son, Jesus. Amen.

EPHESIANS 1:4, 6:12; JOHN 8:32,44; 2 PETER 1:12

Participate, Believe, and Receive

God knew you before he formed you in your mother's womb, and he knew your spirit before creation. Life, on life's terms, sidetracked you from his plan. Addiction got you to treatment and prison, with no hope and a bleak future, along with many consequences. Battered, bruised, and believing the enemy's lies, you manipulated your next fix to medicate the pain deep within. You fought constantly with yourself, and others, when the war was really between you and the devil. Your choices, made in your heart, planned your course.

God allowed you to stumble down your road with blinders on. After finally reaching total brokenness, you fought to live: "Lord, I beg you to save me. Deliver me from this hell on earth." God answered and set you into recovery for you to participate, believe, and receive by faith. His plans are for you to prosper, not come to harm, with hope and a future. It's difficult to be what you don't know, and you don't know how to be a man, until you see a man. It's critical to learn from a man who's walking out their faith, in sobriety.

Lord, I need men to watch and learn from, who are walking out their faith in sobriety. Please remind me, constantly, to follow the steps you determined for me. Amen.

JEREMIAH 1:5, 29:11; PROVERBS 16:9

Recovery Season

Solomon, with all his wisdom, discovered there's a time to plant, and to harvest; a time for everything, and a season for every activity under Heaven. Your season of recovery is now! God invites you to climb through this window of opportunity, and he will provide everything you need to succeed.

You begin with baby steps, led by the Spirit, to make practical application of God's Word to your circumstances. Jesus, the good shepherd, opens the gate of recovery and calls you to lead you out from the life of bondage to addiction, into his protection.

You have struggled with your true purpose, wondering if pain and shame was all there was. The thief's purpose is to steal, kill, and destroy you; the good shepherd's purpose is that you have life in abundance. Where purpose is not known, abuse is inevitable. You were convinced you were less than nothing and unworthy of any good thing. God wants you to see your true value in him.

Lord, thanks for my time and season of recovery. I choose, today, to respond to the shepherd's voice. I desire to be victorious. Amen.

Ecclesiastes 3:1-2; John 10:3, 10; 1 Thessalonians 5:18

Increase Your Faith

The Messiah endured the violence of the cross to cleanse you with his blood, make you right with the Father, and cancel all debt against you. In a radical display of trust, you can leave the enemy camp of destruction to do the good things God planned for you long ago. Wherever you go, you begin to trust that God's presence goes with you, and you discover green pastures for resting. The Spirit empowers you with the courage to speak to your mountains.

Apart from Christ, you've settled for crumbs on the floor. There are only two voices: the father of lies, and the Father of truth. Lies equal death. Truth is life.

You receive the Holy Spirit through faith by hearing the Word of God. It's your choice to increase your faith, not God's. The sweat equity that increases faith is to begin speaking words of life over yourself and your circumstance. A powerful, spiritual exchange takes place when your ears hear your lips speaking words of life (truth) over yourself.

Jesus, I believe in my heart you're the risen Lord; thanks for saving me from myself. I desire for my ears to hear my lips speaking your words of life. Amen.

PSALM 23; EPHESIANS 2:10; MARK 11:23; ROMANS 8:6

Spirit and Life

The words you speak over yourself, or others, are liberating or incarcerating! You'll eat the fruit of words spoken and always reap what you sow. With child-like faith, you know the Word's near you; it's in your mouth and in your heart.

The heart believes and you're justified; your mouth confesses and you're saved. The enemy hates when you speak the truth; he is out to steal God's Word from you—it's intense spiritual warfare! Abraham, the father of faith, was convinced of God's promises, and he believed in the unseen.

Jesus asked his Father, at the Last Supper, to protect the disciples from the evil one. God wants to be involved in your recovery. He waits for you to open your door so he can teach you the truth. You don't need to continue embracing insanity, or experience another relapse. God sends his angels to work on your behalf.

Lord, I'm grateful your words of truth are spirit and life. I pray my words decrease and your words spoken through me increase. Amen.

GALATIANS 6:7; ROMANS 10:8; JOHN 6:63, 17:17; PSALM 103:20

Content with Today

There will be days that shame makes it difficult to forget the former things and not dwell on the past. Gratitude for God's unconditional love, the reason you're still breathing, chases shame out of the house. God lifted you to a place of safety, and his power now flows through you to help others lost in addiction.

Only by God's grace do you accept your nothingness, and find strength to seek him first in all things. It's a blessing to remember your desperation and gratitude for God's deliverance.

God needs your participation to activate his promises in your life. He will teach you how to apply his principles and receive his blessings. You can do all things through Christ who gives you strength, and be content to live on almost nothing. It's easy to get twisted when you are focused on tomorrow or next week. You don't need to be anxious about that! Take it one day at a time. As focus on tomorrow decreases, time in his presence today increases.

Lord, I watch in hope, wait for you, and know you'll hear me.
I pray tomorrow does not steal today. Amen.

ISAIAH 43:18; PHILIPPIANS 4:13; LUKE 11:3; MATTHEW 6:34; MICAH 7:7

Everyone Is Recovering

Everyone on this planet is recovering from something. A mustard seed of willingness is all that's needed to take a step out of addiction and enter God's unique witness-protection program. Fixed on your next fix, the only peace you thought possible was death. During life's most violent storm, your ship's mast was ripped away while you were sinking. Absolutely nothing could help you except God, and he heard your cry.

God lifted you from your impending watery grave, set your feet on a firm place, and enrolled you in his accelerated program of faith, grace, and mercy. If you stumble, you won't fall; he upholds you with his hand.

The prodigal son was full of guilt and shame even though his father loved and received him back into his home. Guilt, remorse, and regret keep you from receiving the heavenly Father's welcome. Get over yourself and walk into his embrace.

Lord, I pray I will see myself as you see me. I pray for courage to receive your welcome home. Amen.

PSALMS 37:23-24, 40:2; LUKE 15:21-22

Put Off the Old Self

When God's truth begins to shine, you have choices to make. Begin by confronting the person you've become with honesty and without justification, excuses, or blame. The old self is your evil nature and former way of life—rotten through and through.

It's a game changer when you know God has a purpose for your life. He desires to save others through you and share his message of hope to the hopeless. As God's Spirit renews your thoughts and attitudes, you begin to embrace the new self. Don't let the enemy trick you into thinking it's up to you to change. It's an inside job! Stay out of God's way, and lay your addiction at Jesus' cross.

You will have thoughts of returning to your addiction at times, and even dreams of medicating again; yet, the Spirit empowers you to not act on those thoughts or dreams. Let your new self make your decisions today.

Lord, I pray for your grace to search, give up, and throw away the old self in me. I praise you for this new day and for a new me. Amen.

EPHESIANS 4:22-24; ECCLESIASTES 3:6

Housecleaning

After stumbling into recovery and confronting past choices, you begin to experience emotional sobriety as well as physical clean time. Many started this journey because of someone's persistence or legal consequences. Your false promises of never using again were no longer believed.

If you don't learn to stand for something, you're going to keep falling for anything. If you don't persist in pursuing the Lord with the energy you used to pursue your addiction, your recovery is in danger.

God brought you up from the grave, and spared you from going down into the pit. He desires to begin your emotional and spiritual housecleaning from the years of bondage to your addiction. Ego and pride will not go down without a struggle and will attempt to continue making decisions for you. It's essential to have accountability with someone who will teach you to identify the triggers the enemy uses to disrupt your spiritual, emotional, and physical healing.

Lord, I desire to respect, follow, and serve you, and be prompt in responding to your nudges. I submit to my emotional and spiritual housecleaning. Amen.

PSALM 30:2-3; JEREMIAH 3:15; DEUTERONOMY 10:12

Purchased Freedom

The enemy specializes in shame, guilt, and rejection. For many years, he twisted you to medicate for relief from yesterday's broken road, today's anxious thoughts, and your fear of tomorrow. God's truth declares you're forgiven for yesterday, you're strengthened for today, and he holds your future in his hands.

Trust that he's never forgotten, forsaken, or given up on you. He keeps watch over you. Be grateful for this day that you're alive, breathing, above ground, and out of prison. God's gift of his Spirit empowers you to leave the battlefield in your mind and walk in his wisdom. When the enemy comes to condemn you, God declares there's no condemnation.

You're no longer a victim, full of self-pity, a miserable failure, or a condemned prisoner on death row. If a child falls into a mud puddle, do you throw away the dirty child or just wash the dirty clothes? God purchased you through the blood of his Son, and your robe has been washed so it's sparkling white.

Jesus, I'm so grateful you washed my sins away with your blood. I pray you continue to wash life's dirt and nastiness off me on a daily basis. Amen.

PSALM 121:8; ROMANS 8:1; EPHESIANS 1:7; REVELATION 1:5

Confess and Be Healed

Your recovery depends on dealing with the grunts, groans, and murmuring that became your primary language. How often did you refuse to confess your addiction even while your body was wasting away? Everyone on this planet, at some time, has agreed with the enemy's lies and kept their secrets and frustrations locked inside.

You murmur and groan, justify, make excuses, and continually rehearse the Top Ten Reasons you don't need to confess or bring things into the light. This seed, seemingly small, can become huge, opening the door to chaos and another relapse.

Anger always overflows onto others. Anger and misery separate you from God and others. You end up in extreme loneliness because you push people away. Renew your health with strength that comes from fearing the Lord, and turn away from evil. Confess and don't quit!

Lord, I confess my sins and am deeply sorry for my groans and murmuring. Come quickly to help me, O Lord! Amen.

Psalms 32:3, 38:3, 18, 22; Proverbs 3:7-8

Who Condemns You?

God's light reveals the sin within you that keeps sabotaging your best intentions; in fact, your best intentions couldn't keep you out of the liquor store, crack house, or casino. You agreed with the enemy's lie of being unworthy of a life of peace, and think you deserve punishment for the guilt of your past. You became your own opponent: a subtle self-destruction of hopelessness and shame. The slippery slope of self-condemnation kept the resentments building and depression deepening.

Oh, what a miserable person! Who will free you from this life dominated by addiction? Only the name of Jesus, and his action of love on the cross delivers you from the slick, double-dealing liar's condemnation, despair, and gloom.

Jesus' lush, green meadows and white daisies of faith, hope, and love, await you. God exchanges the slippery slope for his firm foundation and the roller coaster of emotions with wisdom. Who then condemns you? Christ Jesus? No! Jesus died, was raised to life, and pleads for you while seated next to his Father. All you need to do is trust.

Lord, I'm grateful I didn't get what I deserved, and that you set my feet in a spacious place. I pray for courage to embrace more fully the power of your name. Amen.

ROMANS 7:17-18, 7:24-25, 8:34; PSALM 31:8

Another Chance

Our faith may fail, yet God remains faithful. Even though you turn your back on him, he always remains at your side. In the darkest days of addiction with your depression and manic-bipolar disorder racing endlessly in the darkness of the psych ward, seeking relief in all the wrong places, and thinking suicide was the only option—God was faithful! How do you know? You're still alive with the miracle of another chance at recovery.

When gimpy legs can no longer stand, God gives you special favor in Christ to be strong. His undeserved favor and grace takes you to a new dimension of trusting and living in his power, rather than yours. You can never do enough to qualify for his blessings, grace, or tender mercies. Only God qualifies you, and he chooses to because it gives him great pleasure.

Instead of the need to control, you endure suffering as a soldier in Christ's army. Don't get twisted with what's going on around you; focus and tell another who is still suffering that God is faithful.

Lord, I'm grateful you saved me from the enemy's torture.
Thanks for being faithful even when I was faithless. Amen.

2 TIMOTHY 2:3-4, 13

Use God's Armor

A soldier in service follows the orders of the ranking officer and is on high alert for the enemy. When setting up camp, the first duty is to prepare the perimeter to defend against the enemy. A good soldier will follow orders to carry out the mission and leave no one behind.

Strong leaders always surround themselves with strong warriors who perfect their skills and are mentally tough, determined, and dedicated to serve to the best of their ability. You've proven yourself to be a warrior.

Every day, you're engaged in spiritual warfare and you're subject to Satan's attacks. The mind that got you into the enemy's bamboo cage of addiction cannot get you out. You need reliable and faithful drill instructors to instruct and teach you to be an alert soldier. Don't get twisted with civilian affairs. There will be opposition. If tortured by the enemy, endure everything for the sake of God's chosen. Use God's armor to resist the devil, so after the battle you'll still be standing firm.

Lord, I pray for the courage to be a good soldier for you. I pray to remain faithful when tortured by the enemy. Thanks for your armor. Amen.

2 TIMOTHY 2:10, 3; EPHESIANS 6:13-17

Reserved Seat

You've sold yourself short so many times because of guilt and unworthiness. You're totally unaware of the baggage that came with you entering recovery: deeply rooted dependencies, suppressed memories, and resentments. Yes, God's got them. He renews and transforms your mind. The bondage that held you captive had become your way of life—insanity became your normal. You've carried the enemy's lies around for years; recovery is a time to dump the baggage.

God's got your reserved seat at his banquet table, and you don't need to be under the table looking for crumbs. God invites you to take your rightful place at his table. He is the bread of life.

Jesus' bread is a seed of love from the Father, who gives food to those who trust him. God says you're worthy to take a seat at his table. He has already reserved it for you and is celebrating your homecoming. Welcome!

Lord, I'm eternally grateful to eat your bread of life. Thanks for reserving a seat for me at your table. Amen.

LUKE 15:23-24; JOHN 6:35

The Son Will Set You Free

In recovery you have the choice to set your mind on the flesh or the Spirit; the flesh is death, and the Spirit is life and peace. St. Paul struggled with sin as you do—he found it hard not to do the things his flesh wanted him to do. In addiction the enemy deceived you with his counterfeit truth: a devious strategy of impersonation by the enemy. You medicated your pain and shame with your addiction.

Your corrupt nature is opposed to your spiritual nature. That's why you don't do what you intend to do. You need people who love you enough to confront, not coddle, your behavior when you stumble and trip over the sin inside you. You need to be reminded that when Jesus died, the power of sin died with him.

Despite whatever's going on, overwhelming victory is yours through Christ, who loves you. Jesus liberates you from death and slavery. It took a free man to free a man. And you are indeed free!

Lord, I choose to set my mind on you. I'm grateful you set me free, and I desire to free another who is lost in addiction. Amen.

Romans 7:17, 20, 8:6, 37; Galatians 5:17; John 8:36

More Important

When you think you're really something, the enemy's deceit has twisted you once again. The false facade of thinking others are less important is a setup to avoid confronting your own faults. This critical and condemning spirit has to do with entitlement and feelings of superiority. The mask of self-importance is violently ripped off each time you dare to admit you're poor in spirit.

When connected to something greater than yourself, you begin to uncover all that's been a hindrance to accept yourself as you truly are: one of God's children. When you reveal to God and yourself that you're a ragged child in dire need of God's grace and mercy, the blessing you receive is that you will judge yourself and others less harshly.

There's a time coming when everything that's covered up will be revealed, and all secrets will be made known to all. To jumpstart your healing, tell on yourself. God gives you the opportunity to practice his powerful principle of acceptance. In humility, consider others better than yourself.

Lord, I pray for humility to know others are as important to you as I am. I pray for courage to confront my self-centered false self. Amen.

GALATIANS 6:3; LUKE 12:2; PHILIPPIANS 2:3

Remember When He Saved You

It's essential to remember the day God saved you from the enemy's trap of addiction. In dire poverty, lame, blind, paralyzed, anxious, panic-stricken, paranoid, with body and soul withering away, God deployed his angels to hunt you down and set you in a safe place. Hurtful words defined you, while immense fear of loneliness and depression were draining your strength.

The enemy demands blood self-sacrifice: judgment and punishment decreed from the pit of hell. Your sad existence may have almost ended when coming into agreement with the enemy's sentence. God stepped in at the last possible second to save your life.

Let his living Word encourage you to draw near to him with a sincere heart. Start asking God for the ability to transition from blaming others to admitting you did it to yourself. The Father sprinkles your heart to cleanse your guilty conscience and wash your body with his living water. Do you remember?

Lord, thanks for your gift of child-like faith. I praise you for sacrificing your life for mine. Help me to always remember when you saved me. Amen.

Psalm 31:8-10; Luke 3:11; Hebrews 10:23

Recovery Is Possible

Recovery is possible for you, even after multiple treatments and prison time. God invites you to seek him first above all else. He gives you everything you need to make your impossibility, possible! He didn't come to make bad people good, he came to make dead people alive, and to change what you hunger and thirst for. A bit of faith, as tiny as a mustard seed, is all that's needed. Leave your throne to kneel before his.

The disciples couldn't help a young boy possessed by an evil spirit, yet his father never gave up. In desperation, he brought him to Jesus, asking Jesus to do something *if he could*. Of course Jesus could bring healing to the man who believed.

If you believe, your recovery into freedom is possible. When today's troubles scream that recovery isn't possible, know that it is—with God. Don't give up!

Lord, I pray for courage to believe that recovery is possible. I believe I can put my head on the pillow tonight grateful for another day of sobriety and clean time. Amen.

MATTHEW 6:33, 19:26; HEBREWS 11:1; MARK 9:22-23

A New Lawyer

When walking in God's light, the blood of his Son cleanses you from all sin, because of his unfathomable and unconditional love. It's essential to hear stories of how his love cleansed others, and to learn to live by observing their actions. People who embrace the love of the Father love themselves and others; they are great people to be around. When you feel low, you need people who reach into your heart to extract your newly discovered love of Jesus.

The Word declares his love always protects, trusts, hopes, and perseveres. The Father has ruthlessly and aggressively pursued your heart to have fellowship with him. You knew about God, but never knew who he truly was—you were misinformed by misinformed people.

Whenever the devil brings your legal case to heaven's court for a guilty verdict, God asks if someone will represent you. Jesus stands quickly, "I will, Father; in fact, my blood shed on the cross cancelled all debt." God's proud of how well his Son represented you, and he declares throughout the universe, "Not guilty!"

Lord, I'm grateful that instead of shame and dishonor, I'll inherit a double portion of prosperity and everlasting joy. I'm thankful you desire me to remain in your love. Amen.

1 JOHN 1:7; 1 CORINTHIANS 13:7; ISAIAH 61:7; JOHN 15:9

Greater and Less

John the Baptist's reply, when asked if he was the Christ, was simply that he was unworthy to untie the straps of Jesus' sandals. After Jesus was baptized, the Spirit descended on him like a dove. A voice from heaven said, "This is my Son, whom I love; with him I am well pleased." You must become less, for the Lord to become greater.

The significance of this earth-shattering event continues with Jesus asking you to join his story: make it your story and leap onto his train of grace to your eternal destination. When the Holy Spirit nudges you to remove that which hinders and holds you back, what's your response?

Fight through your busy mind and the enemy's resistance to throw off that which threatens your recovery. If it was important for John the Baptist to become less, it's critical for you, too.

Lord, I pray for courage to become less, so you become greater. I'm grateful you came to take away my sin and give me your Spirit. Amen.

JOHN 1:27-30, 3:30; MARK 1:8-10; MATTHEW 3:17

No Shortcuts

Out of extreme weariness and sick of being sick and tired, you finally responded to God's irrevocable call. Think of what you had become and where he called you from—no one thought you wise by human standards. God opened a door of recovery for you that no one else can close, and he chose you in spite of your brokenness. Pursue your recovery with the relentless energy you pursued your addiction. Shortcuts are setbacks.

The roller coaster of emotions, condemnation, and shame are a challenge; you can be on the mountaintop and fall into the valley in an instant. But that's okay; you can now deal with the feelings that have been suppressed for years by bringing them to the light.

Don't become weary in recovery, for at the proper time, you'll reap a harvest. God delivered you from the burning fiery furnace and will also rescue you from the stranglehold of shame.

Lord, thanks for transforming me from a loser into a champion, and from a self-centered, egomaniac into a servant. I'm amazed you selected me so you could love others through me. Amen.

1 CORINTHIANS 1:26-27; REVELATION 3:8; GALATIANS 6:9; DANIEL 3:17

Love the Unlovable

God heard your cry when you admitted you were a mess, drowning in the lifeless cesspool of addiction. He strategically gave you the opportunity to go boldly to the heavenly throne and confront the activities of your flesh. God first loved you, and now he invites you to let him love another suffering addict through you. Love with God's perfect love.

By loving others, you learn to love yourself. It's not easy to love those who, by their actions, irritate and hurt you. You need to confront your reaction and response. Anyone who doesn't love others does not know God. Dishonor others, become easily angered, and nurse resentments, and you will push the recovery destruct button.

It's essential to share God's unconditional love with people— even those you feel are not deserving. They're as unworthy and undeserving as you once were.

Lord, thanks for the wisdom to know you still love me even when I feel guilty, condemned, and judged; I praise you for loving me when I was unlovable. I praise you for your love. Amen.

PSALM 40:1; 1 CORINTHIANS 13:5; 1 JOHN 4:8

Words of Fire

God's Word burns like fire. A mighty hammer that smashes rocks to pieces sounds a bit scary. You got hammered on the streets, so trust it's okay to get hammered by God in recovery. God might show up with a fifty pound sledge hammer to smash the huge boulder of stubborn resistance to his plan for you. God also shakes your tree until all that's left will be fruit that lasts.

Your child-like faith knows recovery is a lifestyle change. You need to be watching and listening for God's direction. A pastor's message, a speaker, your accountability partner, and even the radio can deliver messages that speak directly to you and your circumstance. His Word activates your recovery, and when you can't see the way, it's a reminder—he is the only way.

It's difficult for egomaniacs and self-centered manipulators to ask for help. Your recovery goes much better when you seek counsel, and with many godly advisors it will succeed.

Lord, thanks for the advisors you have given me to receive counsel from. I'm grateful your hammer is so much better than addiction's hammer. I pray for open ears to hear whenever your words of fire come. Amen.

Jeremiah 23:29; Psalm 5:3; John 15:16; Hebrews 4:12; Proverbs 15:22

Life God's Way

Your recovery is about fellowship with God the Father, and an intimate relationship with his Son, Jesus. God knows what you've done during the dark days of seeking the enemy's false promise for relief. The light in the darkness is the brightness of the glory of God, seen in the face of Jesus Christ. Addiction now becomes a great blessing because slavery and bondage brought you to the end of yourself. The Holy Spirit's still, quiet voice can now be heard above the enemy's incessant chatter.

God won't push you away in spite of all you've done; instead, he draws you to himself and reminds you it's not about you. It's all about what he has done for you. God holds the plan for your future, and he takes the unmanageability and powerlessness of your existence to bring order back into it. The key is unrelenting honesty.

Confess your sin of believing the enemy's lie, and accept the truth that God is faithful and just to forgive and cleanse you from everything.

Lord, I'm grateful you took my brokenness and began mending me and making me whole. I'm amazed to know the hands that shaped the world are now holding me. Amen.

2 CORINTHIANS 4:6; JAMES 1:8; 1 JOHN 1:9

It Is Finished

Who will liberate you when stubbornness, ego, and pride want to rule your day? Who guides you to truth when a good decision is needed, and hesitation and doubt blow and toss you around like the wind? Who guards and keeps you in perfect and unwavering peace?

If you're the ultimate authority, you'll always do things your way. God is waiting for you to do it his Way. He gives you wisdom to make good choices, and strengthens you with hope when you intentionally set your mind on him.

Jesus accepts your human frailties and will take your overloaded and overworked mind, washing it with his Spirit. Your flesh and the enemy are a powerful team working against you to control and manipulate decisions, and to steal or kill every blessing. Disarm these forces by bringing your shortcomings to God. He knows your heart and his covering is sufficient. Your sins have been forgiven because of Jesus. He is your advocate, and he reminds you of his last words on the cross: "It is finished."

Lord, give me strength to fight to keep Jesus the center of my life. I'm grateful your sacrifice on the cross was sufficient to erase my past, give me courage for today, and restore hope for my future. Amen.

JAMES 1:6, 5:16; ISAIAH 26:3; 1 JOHN 2:12; JOHN 19:30

God Values Humility

God values you when you show humility and deep sorrow for having done wrong. Pride and ego continually seek control. When admitting you're in dire need of God's grace to go another step, his grace empowers you to continue recovery—the journey to freedom. God's Word sustains and reminds you that everything that comes at you is from him, or allowed by him for your good. No longer lost or abandoned, you have been called for his purpose.

Your recovery's in danger when you muddle in the muck and mess of what's going on around you. Recovery has to be your focus and cause, not a casual commitment or some religious resolve for change. Even though you're ready and willing to break from your addiction, you're not going to let go easily because that lifestyle has been comfortable and familiar.

Only God can do the radical work to come against your great love affair of self. He allowed the consequences of your choices to bring you to brokenness. Instead of blaming everything and everybody for your behavior, you finally admit, "I did this to myself." Let go and let God.

Lord, I'm grateful for your never ending grace. I pray you continue the radical work already begun in me. Amen.

ISAIAH 66:2; JOHN 3:16; ROMANS 8:28

Circle of Respect

When you begin showing respect to others, you'll receive it in return. Respect is showing honor and consideration, which is a challenge when the enemy's paranoia has twisted you to believe everybody is out to get you. You show God great honor when offering your body as a living sacrifice. Each day in recovery is a huge spiritual act of worship.

Don't hold yourself in high esteem; only measure yourself by the faith God's given you. Honest evaluation of self says we fall short daily and are in dire need of God's grace.

You demonstrate honor of Abba Father every time you respect your spiritual leaders. God has placed these people in your life for you to imitate their faith. A pastor, spouse, mentor, or friend are resources to guide you and offer correction when you get off track. Don't be misled when the enemy attempts to twist godly correction to appear as rejection. It's not.

Lord, I pray a blessing over those you've given me to imitate their faith. I desire to meet people where they are—friend or foe—and take delight in honoring them. Help me love others with genuine affection. Amen.

ROMANS 12:1, 3, 10; HEBREWS 13:7

Past Pain or Future Grace?

Your pilgrim's journey begins when you believe God is bigger than anything you face, endure, or suffer through. Addiction enslaved you with chains of your own making, which kept you from loving God or yourself. Don't you know you become a slave to what you chose to obey? God's refined you in the furnace of suffering to choose him and identify the why behind the what.

No one likes to suffer unless they're a slave to self-pity. You want to sit in a comfy recliner when going through God's refining. Yet, without persevering through the testing and trials that come daily, your faith life would be as a fig tree with no fruit.

The test today is to forget what's behind and strain toward what's ahead. You're worthy to embrace the grace for another day in recovery.

Lord, I pray for the courage to give you my shame and pain, rather than medicating with addiction. I pray to continue my recovery by embracing your grace for my future, one day at a time. Amen.

ROMANS 6:16; ISAIAH 48:10; PHILIPPIANS 3:13

Endurance Builds Character

When experiencing problems and trials, it's okay to ask: *Why me?* You're human and you will experience hissy-fits. In recovery, you confront these moments rather than run from them. Rejoice during them because they're good for you—they teach endurance.

God uses your suffering, past pain, difficulties, disasters, and even Satan's attacks to build character and to rekindle your excitement in knowing each new day holds great promise. In God, your future is secure, but without this painful process, there's no progress.

God takes you through it to get to the place he desires you to be. *Reputation* is the way others see you, but *character* is who you really are. Character is an inside job. You'll be known for who you are. Focus on character, and your reputation takes care of itself. Character strengthens during problems and trials, as well as endurance.

Lord, anticipating hope with darkness fading, I pray to persevere and endure. Talent without character is wasted. I pray to see your bright light in the night. Amen.

ROMANS 5:3; JAMES 1:4; PSALM 16:8

True Purpose

Early on in recovery, can you trust that God's got your day? Only God can turn your eyes from worthless things and preserve your life according to his Word. Your purpose was twisted to deliberately and intentionally focus on the next fix, with the expectation that you would be fulfilled. It was a lie from the pit of hell.

Addiction took you to places you never wanted to go, and medicating your pain and shame locked you into a life without true purpose. Take comfort, because while you were lost, God's promise rescued you from addiction.

The enemy kept yelling, "You're a failure, unworthy of any good thing." Your flesh jumped all over this with, "I've got this. I don't need any help, and will do it my way!" You got stuck in the kill zone of this spiritual crossfire while searching for what only God could give you. His words give light and understanding to those who admit they're poor in spirit. Cry out to God, and allow him to fulfill his purpose for you.

Lord, I'm thankful my life now has a purpose. I want to fulfill your purpose for me. I pray I will trust you more. Amen.

PSALMS 57:2, 119:37, 50, 130

God Knows Your Purpose

Your best intentions, along with reasoning and thinking, kept you empty and unfulfilled. Sick and tired of your poverty, you finally experienced a light-bulb moment and realized how destructive your life style had become. Self-sufficiency brought you to self-deficiency.

God's showing you that life is totally impossible to control, or manipulate. According to his promise, the refreshing breath of his Spirit and his unfailing love is your comfort. The Lord created you for his definitive purpose, and he works out every detail.

The inventor knows the purpose of his invention, and since you didn't invent yourself, you can't know your purpose. God knows, and he chose you before you were born. Trust, with child-like faith, that nothing in your past disqualifies you from his purpose. Like the prodigal son, your heavenly Father gathers you in, embraces you tightly, and lovingly qualifies you as one of his kids.

Lord, thanks for accomplishing your purpose so I can discover mine. Your purpose was to bring life and peace; I stand in awe of your name. Amen.

PSALM 119:76; PROVERBS 16:4; ROMANS 10:4; MALACHI 2:5

Let No One Take Your Crown

Only God can be in charge of your recovery. Submit to his authority and hold on to the blessing of another chance, so that no one can take it from you. So much energy is spent doing things your way, yet God tenderly brings you back to his way. You can make many plans, but the Lord's purpose will prevail. God took your hand into his to guide you out from the shadow of death, and place your feet onto the path of peace.

The enemy plans to steal your crown, and replace it with the counterfeit one worn for many years while sitting on the throne of your kingdom of one. You're worthy of wearing the crown that can't get smoked up, drank up, gambled away, rusted out, or stolen.

Be encouraged to hold onto what you've been given. Even if your faith and spiritual strength is little, and your recovery is new, hang on tightly to what God has given you to live for him. Fight to place your head on the pillow tonight, sober and clean. He will bless you for your efforts.

Lord, I pray for the courage to hang onto the crown you placed on my head, and let go of the enemy's counterfeit. Amen.

REVELATION 3:11; PROVERBS 19:21; LUKE 1:79

Garments that Last for Eternity

Jesus purchased new garments for you with his blood. He clothed you with the garments of salvation, covering you with his robe of righteousness. In recovery, you're beginning to embrace your journey, yet you wonder, at times, if his garments fit properly, or if his robe covers you sufficiently.

The enemy urges you to not put your big toe into God's living water. Only when realizing your life depends on it, do you dare to run off the end of the dock and take the leap of faith into his waters of life.

You are clothed and covered by the great designer; he makes a way in the sea whenever the storms of life come, a path through the mighty waters when the waves rise higher and higher. The enemy's counterfeit truth is that you don't have enough faith for a full recovery. Is your faith strong enough? How much faith did Lazarus have when dead in the grave? God says you only need faith as small as a tiny mustard seed. Regardless of where you are, you have more faith than Lazarus did.

Lord, I love the eternal warranty on your garments. I pray for wisdom to know any faith I have is sufficient for you. Amen.

ISAIAH 43:16, 61:10; LUKE 17:6

Judging Others

It takes no effort to judge others by outward appearance, yet the Lord looks at a person's thoughts and intentions. When you walk a few steps in someone's shoes, then you can exchange having an opinion about them for compassion for them. God gives discernment to see they're hurting and doing the best they can, just like you.

As you embrace your poverty of spirit, in dire need of the Father's love, you accept others as also needing the Father's love. You only judge when you're under judgment.

During addiction, the heart becomes calloused and hard. Without living water it will never spring back to life. You were misused and abused by the enemy's constant attacks, and you felt unworthy of any good thing in the busyness between your ears. Each time, your heartbeat grew more faint. Just before it ceased to beat, you cried to God to hear your prayer, and be merciful. And God responded. Instead of judging others, you now speak words of life into them.

Lord, I'm grateful to know when judging others I'm really judging myself with a critical spirit, which isn't from you. Thanks for my new heart. Amen.

1 SAMUEL 16:7; PSALM 27:7; EZEKIEL 36:26

A Fresh Start

God's gift of a new tender, responsive heart offers you a fresh start and new beginning, regardless of what you've done. He sprinkles living water to clean and wash away all your filth. Why patch up the old life when you can have a new one? As you embark on this marvelous journey, God begins restoring you physically and spiritually. His Spirit empowers you to pursue a more profound, personal relationship with your Lord and Savior. Jesus, while holding your new heart in his hands, deletes the devil's programming of your life's computer, and downloads his Spirit into you.

As Jesus fills you with himself, you receive the greatest bonus on this planet, without asking, or being qualified—his audacious gift of replacing the defective blood with the very blood he shed on the cross.

God directs your heart into his love and Christ's perseverance. Are your thoughts and intentions today in line with his? A tender, responsive heart submits to God's love. He equips you for his purpose, and strengthens you to stay another day.

Lord, I pray for the courage to say yes, to a new, fresh start. I pray to be willing for you to love another addict through me. Amen.

EZEKIEL 36:25-26; 2 THESSALONIANS 3:5

Guard Your Heart

Keep your heart with all diligence, and be vigilant, alert, and careful as you guard it because everything you do flows from it. Everything said, or done to you, and all you've said or done to others is stored in your heart. Your heart runs your life, and it is deceitful above all things and desperately wicked.

The condition of the heart determines the course of your life, and in order to protect the new transplanted, tender, responsive heart, and stay on course, you need to operate effectively on the level God has placed you.

When your heart becomes hardened, you don't even think, say, or do the things you intend to do. You need to ask the Holy Spirit for regular check-ups on your heart's condition, to keep it tender and responsive. Your flesh hates the Holy Spirit check-ups, and the enemy always lies about your heart's condition. The Father strengthens you to be vigilant, and declares you're worthy to take care of your new tender heart until you come face to face with Jesus.

Lord, I ask for strength to guard the new heart you placed in me. I'm thankful to know all the issues of life are my issues. Amen.

PROVERBS 4:23; JEREMIAH 17:9

Childish Things

When you embrace knowing your heart, you begin to be aware of your reactions to situations and circumstances. When your emotion takes charge, you often say words to other people you regret having said. When you operate under your own strength, and let your mind do the talking, there's trouble looming on the horizon—that's just the way it is. You don't have all the answers now, but one day you will. Don't give up!

In recovery, you start a new life as a babe in Christ. When you're a child, you speak, think, and reason like a child; yet, when you grow up, you put aside childish things. What you know now is partial and incomplete. Be encouraged; this is a journey and there will be bumps in the road. When you look in the mirror and it's still a bit foggy, remember, soon things will be clearer as you see them through God's eyes.

Your recovery is a work in progress, and as you submit to God's Spirit for guidance, your emotional response is being replaced by wisdom and knowledge—one day at a time.

Lord, I pray to trust you with my recovery and pour out my heart to you; for you are my refuge. Amen.

PROVERBS 4:23; 1 CORINTHIANS 13:11-12; PSALM 62:8

Stand on What God Says

You must keep in touch with the condition of your heart, and respond when the Holy Spirit whispers a warning that your heart has grown stony and stubborn. It's a gentle reminder of your need to keep your heart tender and obedient.

It begins with a decision, continues with self-examination, and culminates when you admit a major overhaul of your heart is essential to have God's Spirit within you. When Jesus' blood begins flowing through your veins and arteries, your prayer becomes, "Create in me a pure heart, O God, and renew a steadfast spirit within me."

You begin to stand on what God says and not on what you think or say. His Word never changes; your mind and will can change in a second. Be on guard to not let your emotions be your first response. Regardless of what others might say, stay focused on following Jesus no matter the cost. When you hear God's Word, cling to it, as it will patiently produce a huge harvest. The blessing is that you have God's Word and your testimony, and that's all you need for this day.

Lord, I'm thankful you delight in my efforts, and make my steps firm. I pray for strength for passing life's tests, so they become my testimony. Amen.

EZEKIEL 36:26-27; PSALMS 37:23, 51:10; LUKE 8:15

God's Gentle Whisper

You need to examine why it's so easy to listen to the devil, and so difficult to listen to God. There will be opposition presented to keep your heart from receiving what God has for you. The devil attempts to confuse and distract you from listening to what the Spirit of God is saying because he doesn't want you to hear the Father's still, quiet voice.

God's wisdom enlightens your mind to be able to understand and apply his Word in a practical way to your everyday life. This is about progress, not perfection, and the Father's there when you walk unsteadily. Though you may stumble, you will not fall.

It's essential for your recovery to hear and receive what God says. Jesus withdrew from crowds of people when he wanted to talk with his Father; so leave the loud, wild party room between your ears and focus on getting into Jesus' lap. His Spirit empowers you to hear clearly.

Lord, I pray you will guard and keep me in perfect peace when my mind is focused on you. My heart's desire is to hear your voice. Amen.

JOHN 8:43; I CORINTHIANS 2:11; PSALM 37:23-24; ISAIAH 26:3

The Seed

The Bible is a bag of seeds to fulfill your needs, and when you study God's Word, you learn enough about him to not doubt him. The Father desires you to share the light of his truth, which illuminates your path for others still struggling. You're starting over, like a young child taking their first ride on a brand new bicycle. Regardless of what your flesh or the enemy says, God's not dead and he's never late. Don't allow impatience to hurry the process.

You don't need to beat yourself up upon discovering your timing has taken over again. Remember, you didn't choose God; he chose you. Jesus chose to die for you and he invites you to live with him forever.

By God's grace, choose him, and don't give up before the harvest. Today, persevere until your head hits the pillow tonight, regardless of the chaos of the day. You will sleep well and wake up in safety because the Lord watches over you.

Lord, I'm so grateful for peaceful sleep when knowing you're in control of my circumstances. I pray for the strength to persevere to reap the harvest you've set aside for me. Amen.

LUKE 8:11, 18; JOHN 15:16; PSALM 3:5

A Good Soil Person

Take an honest look where you are today when hearing God's living word. A footpath person hears the Word, but the devil comes and steals it away, preventing them from believing and being saved. A rock person hears the message with joy, believes for a while, but in the time of testing falls away. A thorn patch person will hear and accept the message, but it's soon crowded out by the cares, riches, and pleasures of this life. A good soil person, with a noble and good heart, hears God's message and perseveres to produce a crop.

Many leave treatment before any foundation is built; some string together six-to-nine months with glory, alleluias, and in an instant disappear; while others give up before their harvest of blessings, focusing on getting back what they lost, and doing it their way. The distraction of outside influences is a reason and excuse for those who leave recovery early.

Some can qualify for being a footpath, rock, or thorn patch person, and appear to be okay even when miserable. Yet, in recovery, your only hope is to be a good soil person because the other three spell relapse.

Lord, I pray for the courage to be a good soil person. I pray to choose your instruction instead of silver, and knowledge rather than gold. I pray for those who relapse, that they have another recovery. Amen.

LUKE 8:12-15; PROVERBS 8:10

Run with Purpose

God invites you to run with purpose and not waste your time and energy shadowboxing. Your addictive behavior had you running aimlessly, seeking love in all the wrong places, and beating the air. The enemy tricked you into running a marathon with no finish line.

Without purpose, you'll also work your recovery program your way, un-teachable, lacking discipline, and arguing with yourself. You need to be acutely aware of each step, as one wrong step can cancel out the many steps already taken in your new life.

With child-like faith, dare to run with purpose. You've always been a strong starter out of the gate, but after five weeks into recovery it's easy to become complacent and lazy. Your purpose is to please God, not people—including yourself. God alone examines the motives of your heart. It's your choice to lose favor with people, or lose favor with God. Surround yourself with people who will stand together with one spirit and fight with you for the faith.

Lord, I pray for your continued grace to please you, not people. Thanks for my purpose—to carry your message to those still suffering in addiction. Amen.

1 CORINTHIANS 9:26; 1 THESSALONIANS 2:4; PHILIPPIANS 1:27

Words like Honey

People-pleasing is a stronghold, and the desire for acceptance will dramatically compromise your recovery. You've been influenced by other people's drama, cared only about what you could do for them, and it's drained you of any good thing.

When blessed with God's favor, you're brought into fellowship with people who are filled with love that comes from a pure heart, a clear conscience, and genuine faith. Hang with those who meet you where you are, and accept you as you truly are. Run from those speaking words of shame, who entice you to go against your beliefs, and who twist you to do anything to gain their acceptance. Embrace those who speak kind words over you; they're like honey, sweet to the soul, healthy, and healing for your body.

God sends people to teach you wisdom and discipline, guide you, and encourage you to stand fast in God's grace. It's absolutely amazing what you'll experience when working together with others who want to be free. God calls you to recover, so you can help others into recovery.

Lord, I pray for a pure heart, a clear conscience, and genuine faith. Thanks for those who speak words of honey over me. Amen.

1 TIMOTHY 1:5; PROVERBS 1:2, 16:24; 1 PETER 5:12; PHILIPPIANS 2:2

Stay in Recovery

Your flesh hates to respond to God's nudge to go to an unfamiliar place, and step out of the boat. Jesus invited Peter to come to him, "Take courage! Don't be afraid." Peter didn't know what to do. When he left the safety of the boat, the storm frightened him and he began to sink. Peter's doubt kept him from what Jesus asked. You either listen to yourself and stay, or listen to the Word and go.

You've been in the boat of wavering and indecision; you're "in it to win it" when it's smooth sailing, yet you sink when the storm hits. Stay, or go? Your opinion doesn't matter; the truth doesn't adjust itself to you. Ask your counselor, mentor, or family member if you should stay in recovery—their opinion matters.

You never settled for a watered-down drink, why accept a watered-down recovery? Cut-up dope? No way! Why cut up your recovery? You didn't play the penny slots hoping to win big. Why go for just one cent of recovery?

Lord, I desire to pray to you when life is good with the same intensity I prayed when helpless, homeless, or in prison. I'm so grateful you have power to do what you promise. Amen.

MATTHEW 14:27-31; ROMANS 4:21; 1 KINGS 18:21

There Is Time

Everyone on this planet is in recovery from something; yet, it goes a bit deeper for those who are older. The enemy might tell you that you will remain on the prison chain-gang until you die, breaking rocks with a sledge-hammer. The enemy's constant chatter tells you that you've labored for no purpose, all your strength was spent for nothing, and you are out of time. But God says that the rest of your life will be the best of your life.

Child-like faith, the size of a mustard seed, gives renewed hope. When you leave everything in the Lord's hand, God rewards you. You went through all you experienced to get to the place God desired you to be. There's time to start anew. You can do anything in Christ's strength.

It's a good place anytime you reach the end of yourself, because that's when God begins his work in and through you. Jesus is able to save completely those who come to God through him. You have time!

Lord, thanks for allowing me to come to the end of myself. I'm grateful that when I was in darkness, you said, "Come out," and when in captivity, you said, "Be free." Amen.

Isaiah 49:4-9; Philippians 4:13; Hebrews 7:25

Your Purpose

It's difficult, if not impossible, to be miserable when serving others in need, or carrying his message to suffering addicts. Drop everything you're doing, get out of your favorite recliner, and answer a call for help. Thanks be to God, he gave you victory through his Son, Jesus. He took you from being a victim to becoming a victor, and reconciled you to himself through Christ. When you live in Him, He lives in you, and because God brought you into his camp, you can bring another into recovery's camp.

When once you trusted addiction for relief, you now trust God for your reward and purpose. Your purpose needs to match his purpose for you. It's not just to get back what you lost. People of purpose teach you purpose—that it's time to grow up and stop being an over-thinker. That paralyzes you.

In child-like faith, you can receive a pure heart and a clear conscience, which reveals your purpose. You no longer grieve what you lost, but celebrate what you've gained—God's great love!

Lord, thanks for my purpose to carry your message of hope to addicts still suffering. I'm amazed you spared me, and I didn't get what I deserved. Amen.

1 CORINTHIANS 15:57; 2 CORINTHIANS 5:18; 1 TIMOTHY 1:5; 1 JOHN 4:9

Lean on God

Trust is a firm belief in the reliability of a power greater than yourself. The journey into trust begins when a ruffian admits they're impoverished and in dire need of God's grace. It might not *feel* good, but it *is* good. To admit you don't trust your own judgment is an act of humility. You begin focusing on God, the source of your hope, rather than on what others are saying about you. As you trust him more, God fills you completely with joy and peace.

Lean on and trust God. Be confident in him with all your heart and soul. Learn to make decisions that are not from emotions. The bottom line is that you'll eventually have to trust God because you'll mess up without him.

You can't trust or lean on someone you don't know, so get to know the one who knows everything. God invites you to know, recognize, and acknowledge him. Can God trust you with what he's entrusted to you—recovery? It's your choice this day to say, "Yes!"

Lord, I pray to go deeper in my trust for you. I desire my actions to show my trust in you. I don't want to rely on my own understanding. Amen.

1 CORINTHIANS 4:3; ROMANS 15:13; PROVERBS 3:5-6; MATTHEW 5:37

Trust Issues

It's okay to admit you've got trust issues: everyone does. Many experienced an assault or attack from someone in whom they'd placed great trust. The enemy convinced you to keep it secret and hold it deep inside. Yet, this act of violence continues to torture you daily. It's your season to let it go, and trust God. He desires to rescue you from the brutality of the past. You will find new strength to run into your healing.

Jesus invites you to trust him, not yourself. The Spirit gives life; the flesh counts for nothing. God's words are life. He sends people to teach you wisdom and understanding about trust. When you remain faithful to the things you're taught, your trust in the one who is faithful grows.

Remember those who brought the Word of God to you. Even though your trust wavers at times, dare to follow the godly example of those special people, observing how they live. Whatever it takes to get there, just get there!

Lord, I pray to be confident in trusting you, and not quit before the blessing. I pray to remain faithful to what I've been taught. Amen.

ISAIAH 40:31; JOHN 6:63; 2 TIMOTHY 3:14; JEREMIAH 3:15; HEBREWS 13:7

It's Not Complicated

Almighty God wants you to respect him, follow him, love him, and serve him with all your heart and soul. The enemy has twisted you into a complex formula of what you must do, even though Jesus already did it! These four essentials are not complicated: ease up, relax, rest in his lap, and remember it's all about him.

God desires you, to the best of your ability, to allow him to be in charge of the outcome. The Father desires to write his living words on the tablet of your heart. He removed your heart of stone, replacing it with a new heart.

The Father revealed his great love for you by sending his Son to die for you, while you were still dead in sin, to remove your stain of guilt. His blood washed and cleansed you whiter than snow. When Jesus returned to the Father, he sent the Holy Spirit to empower, guide, teach, and declare your future is secure. There will be opposition and trials to test your faith. When God is shaking your tree, that's okay; he's making room for more of him.

Lord, I pray not to get anxious when you're shaking my tree. Thanks, Holy Spirit, for living in me. Thanks, Jesus, for sending the Spirit of truth. Thanks, Father, for sending your Son. Amen.

DEUTERONOMY 10:12; PROVERBS 7:2-3; EZEKIEL 36:26; JOHN 16:13; 1 PETER 1:7

Unlocked

Everything that's ever happened to you is stored in your heart. The enemy twisted you into agreement that certain areas of your heart were restricted and off limits. In fact, after being convinced to lock up those hurts, resentment, and guilt, you gave him the key to those chambers.

In recovery, it's essential to ask God to get back your key and allow him total access to your heart, so his words can penetrate deeply. Your heart affects everything you do. When God begins his heart work, your unworthiness wants to keep him on the main floor. Let him go upstairs; let him have the downstairs. And then with child-like faith, open up every closet, one at a time. Yes, even the hidden one! As you trust in him, Jesus makes his home in your heart.

May your roots grow deep into the soil of God's marvelous, unconditional love. Enjoy your new, tender heart as he fills you with joy and peace.

Lord, thanks for sprinkling my guilt with your blood to cleanse my heart. I pray your love reaches every area, and your blood flows throughout. Amen.

PROVERBS 4:20-23; EPHESIANS 3:17; HEBREWS 10:22

Nurture One Another

God calls you to love him with all your heart, soul, strength, and mind; and to love your neighbor as yourself. Nurturing is love in action. Your addiction destroyed your ability to care for anyone, especially yourself. Your heart valves became obstructed and hindered Jesus' blood flow through you.

Many at an early age came into agreement with the devil's severe judgment of guilt, and feeling unworthy of God's love. They heavily medicated their shame, searching for relief from the pain, as chaos and confusion reigned supreme.

In recovery, you set aside your false pride and ego to receive God's unconditional love. You can't keep it unless you give it away, and love in action is to pass it on to those who are hungry and thirsty. Invite a stranger in, and visit those in prison. Whatever you do for the least, you do for Jesus. Be on guard, and don't become weary in doing good.

Lord, I pray I will receive your love more quickly. I pray for strength to not become weary in doing good. Amen.

LUKE 10:27; MATTHEW 25:37-40; GALATIANS 6:9

Serve One Another

Only God can transform a cold-hearted, selfish ego-maniac into a tender-hearted, selfless, humble servant. If anyone is in Christ, he is new. To be new in Christ is to love him above all else, and to follow him because you must be where he is. The Father will honor you for being of service to the Lord's work.

You are no longer alone; you're now part of the body of Christ. Stay close to his heartbeat, and be where his fruit is evident. Jesus' example of washing the feet of the disciple who betrayed him invites you to wash the feet of the people who have hurt you the most deeply.

It's an absolute stretch; yet, when you were filthy and condemned to die, Jesus took your place to become your sacrifice so you might live. He invites you to love and serve those you consider dirty.

Lord, I pray for the courage when I can't love others, to allow you to love them through me. I pray for grace to have pure motives so my actions will not be hollow. Help me to be God-centered, not self-centered. Amen.

2 CORINTHIANS 5:17; JOHN 12:26; 1 CORINTHIANS 12:27

Respect One Another

The Lord wants you to respect and follow him with all your heart and soul. Are you respecting yourself and those God has placed in your life as authority? There's no authority that exists in your life, except that which God has established.

All on this planet have authority issues. The flesh doesn't like to be told what to do. It doesn't want to take responsibility for its actions, it always wants the easy way, it is impatient, and it loves to make excuses. Authority issues can begin with your earthly father, and will disrupt relationships with your pastor, leadership, loved ones, employers, and teachers.

What God establishes over you absolutely eliminates all the excuses. So in everything, do to others what you would have them do to you. You give proper respect and reverence to God when you treat others with respect.

Lord, I pray you will deliver me from being stubborn and rebellious. I pray to submit to those you have placed in authority over me. Amen.

Deuteronomy 10:12; Romans 13:1; Matthew 7:12; 1 Samuel 15:23

Trust One Another

It's a challenge to trust people because of mistreatment and injury by those you trusted in the past. You built walls for protection so you couldn't be hurt again. God says to trust him, but how can you trust someone you don't know? True trust comes when his Word gets in you.

Trust and follow those who brought to you the Word of God. Observe their example of how they handle themselves. Their validation comes from God, not people. They keep watch over you, to provide the accountability which is key for your recovery.

Don't fall for the enemy's trap of trusting yourself. The Spirit gives life; the flesh counts for nothing. God desires all of you, no holding back. Commit everything you do to the Lord. Trust him, and he will help you.

Lord, I pray for willingness to learn from those you brought to me who speak about you. I pray to be trustworthy and loyal to others. Amen.

JOHN 1:1, 6:63; HEBREWS 13:7,17; PSALM 37:5

Purpose that Prevails

It's a humbling experience when you accept your plans won't work unless they are the Lord's purpose. You might even become grateful for the plans you arranged or devised which didn't work.

Your addiction and self-loathing never allowed you to be content with your present circumstance; they tricked you into dancing the enemy's jig of mapping out your next move. Chaos, guilt, and shame ruled your day as people-pleasing greased the skids to lonely, dark places.

God works all of your experiences out for good when you love him and commit yourself to his purpose. As you accept his purpose for your life, and trust him, all your tests become part of your testimony. Celebrate the day he has planned for you.

Lord, I'm grateful for the many times you protected and saved me from my plans. I'm grateful your purpose prevailed. Amen.

PROVERBS 19:21; ROMANS 8:28

In Due Time

God used your past to get you into recovery alive, breathing, above ground, and out of prison. You experience tender moments when the shepherd makes you lie down in green pastures, and leads you beside still waters.

Some family members don't process your recovery very well. The hurt and betrayal they feel from your past actions can turn them into the self-appointed judge, jury, and executioner. They don't want to hear any more excuses, false promises, or attempts at making amends three weeks into recovery. Focus on remaining steadfast in your recovery, and take the high road. Let your actions speak louder than your words. This takes time.

When you humble yourself, God will lift you up. Your addiction was an evil, violent storm that blew your life's puzzle pieces helter-skelter. Christ reconciled to himself all things. He recovered your broken and dislocated pieces to properly fit together in the tapestry of the abundant life he came to give you. Rejoice!

Lord, I pray you will fit the broken family pieces together and bring your peace. I pray for patience to wait while you do this. Amen.

PSALM 23:1-2; 1 PETER 5:6-7; COLOSSIANS 1:19-20; JOHN 10:10

One Thing to Change

Do you dare ask yourself how sick you really are? Truth was never part of your old lifestyle, and it does not come naturally. You were an expert in the area of destruction, and you need to examine yourself carefully. Jesus Christ is in you! When you begin to get to the root and start dealing with it, it won't be comfortable. Let God begin his good work in you, and be transformed into honesty and transparency. This will save your life.

Your willpower never worked to stop the addictive behavior within you, and each failed attempt took you deeper into despair. In God, you're his handiwork. He has created you for a purpose.

Lacking character will never sustain your new life in recovery. Ask yourself what you need to change. The answer is simple: everything! Everything connected with that old way of life has to go.

Lord, I pray for strength to deal with my character issues before they deal with me. I pray for grace to begin because delay is dangerous, and potentially fatal. Amen.

1 CORINTHIANS 13:5; EPHESIANS 2:10, 4:22

Shield of Faith

When the day's circumstances seem overwhelming, and the thought comes strong whether to stay or leave, you're experiencing a time of testing. The enemy throws flaming darts at you. It's essential to remember your weapons of warfare are not physical. Arm yourself with the shield of faith, which extinguishes the enemy's flaming darts, and the sword of God's word. These are your weapons of choice to use for spiritual warfare.

The Word of God is flawless. Take refuge in God, and he will intervene to shield you from harm and remove the enemy's darts of generational curses. Trust that God can and will do for you what he says.

Your bondage to addiction, and debt for all sins committed, were cancelled when nailed to Christ's cross. He disarmed the evil rulers and shamed them in the most public way, by his victory over them on the cross. Humbly receive your freedom, and climb into his lap to rest.

Jesus, thanks for beating the devil with a big, ugly stick. I pray to use your faith shield, and your sword to fight for my recovery. Amen.

2 CORINTHIANS 10:4; EPHESIANS 6:16; PROVERBS 30:5;
COLOSSIANS 2:13-15

Worship God Forever

God will give you one heart and one purpose—to worship him forever. This is powerful motivation for your recovery because it's no longer just about you. When speaking of purpose, you start with what you know is not God's purpose for you: empty, angry, resentful, depressed, isolated, and miserable. When knowing what your purpose is *not*, you open the door to the truth.

You need to persevere to obtain your purpose, and only God's love activates your faith to be content with where you are today. His love is patient, kind, not boastful or proud, not rude or self-seeking, not easily angered, and keeps no record of wrongs. The Father's love always protects, trusts, hopes, and perseveres.

You no longer have to struggle and waste a lot of time and effort wondering what your purpose is. God has just told you—worship him!

Lord, I pray for the grace to worship you each day I'm alive. Thanks for revealing my purpose to me. Amen.

JEREMIAH 32:29; 1 CORINTHIANS 13:4-7

Don't Become Stagnant

Instant gratification screams at you to graduate with a college degree in perseverance in just a week. I want what I want, when I want it—right now! This is a key driver during addiction. Addiction demanded to get its fix every day regardless of bad weather, no cash, no provider, and an empty gas tank.

You can be grateful the enemy trained you in perseverance with addiction, so you can now use that perseverance in your recovery. The enemy's counterfeit purpose for you was to feed your addiction. Now in recovery, you learn God's purpose by being around people of purpose. Observe those whom God brings into your recovery, strategically, to train you to persevere.

A new day allows you to do more than you did yesterday with your actions, love, faith, and service. Don't become a smelly, stagnant pond; persevere to be a pond with living water flowing in and through.

Lord, I pray to allow perseverance to finish its work in me. I pray each day to do a bit more than yesterday. Amen.

JAMES 1:4; REVELATION 2:19

God's Perfect Love

Are you willing to reveal the fugitives you've harbored, and who you've become? God is working on your behalf, preparing your journey to freedom, and he gives sufficient grace and mercy for the trip. You're no longer on a ship in the middle of the ocean being tossed about during a violent storm. The Father is with you to strengthen, help, and uphold you. He guides you with wisdom, and leads you along straight paths.

As the Father's light illuminates and renews your long lost hopes and dreams, his eternal hope springs forth from you. The enemy's counterfeit is fear: False Evidence Appearing Real. When there's no hope, guilt and shame twist your confused mind to get you to settle for conditional love.

There's no fear in God's love because it is perfect. When fear comes pounding on your door, tell it to leave. As you reflect on the cross Jesus climbed for you, the evidence of his love is absolutely real.

Lord, I pray to go deeper into your love for me. I'm grateful for your perfect love, the gift of your Son. Amen.

GALATIANS 6:3; PROVERBS 4:11; 1 JOHN 4:18

God's Masterpiece

You are God's masterpiece, his greatest work done with masterful skill. Now you can do the good things he planned for you long ago. It's because of his powerful creative work in you that you know this isn't merely for your benefit. The Father desires to use you in mighty and influential ways to speak life into others still lost in addiction. God releases you from the bondage of the dark, forbidden, and lonely closet, so others can see his pleasure shining through you.

God's in the process of restoring you. He wipes off the many layers of shame and guilt with a cloth soaked in the blood of his Son, Jesus. He's preparing you for the great art gallery of the saintly ruffians already saved from addiction, for others to enjoy his pleasure shining upon you.

You cannot rush the process, which has very little to do with you. It's only by God's grace that you are who you are. You are becoming the masterpiece he created you to be—his great work of art.

Lord, thanks for declaring me your masterpiece. I pray to be patient while cleansed by your blood. Amen.

EPHESIANS 2:10; 1 CORINTHIANS 15:10

Where Does Your Help Come From?

When your circumstances overwhelm your spirit and gloom creeps out of the shadows to rest on your shoulders, where do you turn for help? Your first response might be that you should have handled a situation differently and done more, so the day would have been better.

Remember, you're not in charge of the outcome. The Father whispers to you that you're only responsible for the effort. He already knows you'll fall short. Trust him to make up the difference.

The enemy uses the smokescreen of deception to entrap you into believing recovery is totally up to you, and it's measured by the work you put in. Push the reset button and review where your help comes from. When you lift your eyes above your circumstances, you see that your help comes from the Lord. When you approach a challenge, trust the Lord to help you get through it. Don't be afraid of what comes at you; God is watching you.

Lord, I pray to not play the enemy's game of the should-, could-, and would-haves. I pray for grace to look above my situation for your help. Amen.

PSALM 121:1-2, 7-8

Rest in Jesus' Lap

The enemy tricked you into being a people-pleaser, manipulator, and game-player. You did anything to feed the addict inside you. God's unconditional love invites you to rest in him, and find the peace that surpasses all understanding.

Don't attempt to figure this out in the busyness between your ears; you can't. God declared you worthy to salvage and pulled you from the darkness into the light. His peace guards your heart and mind.

Moments in his rest will increase as you keep admitting your need for peace. When he's near, there's no fear! As you rest in his lap a bit longer each time, Jesus reveals more of himself in an extreme, intimate, personal relationship with you. What he has for you far exceeds anything you could ever dream about.

Lord, I'm tired of playing games and desire your rest and peace. I'm so grateful for your light of life. Amen.

PHILIPPIANS 4:7; JOHN 8:12; HEBREWS 13:15

Abba's Child

It is a challenge to wrap your mind around the truth that God adopts us as his children and we get to call him *Abba,* which is like using the word *Daddy.* The Holy Spirit testifies with your spirit that you're one of God's children. Your attempt to figure out some concept of your Father God is limited by your thoughts and influenced by emotions. Only your spirit connects with God's Spirit to discern the truth of who your heavenly Father is.

The Kingdom of God is not what you thought as a child. It is not up in the clouds someplace; it takes root on this planet, beginning with planting tiny, seemingly insignificant seeds. A farmer plants the seed, goes away, and later it sprouts. The Father's in charge of watering and fertilizing the seed, and absolutely nothing on this planet interferes with God's harvest.

As one of God's children, you're to be about some of your Father's business—helping with the harvest of those still suffering.

Lord, I pray to know my Abba Father more intimately. I pray for courage to become a worker for God's harvest. Amen.

ROMANS 8:15-16; MATTHEW 9:37

Extend Your Hand

You are planting seeds and sowing into his Kingdom whenever you allow God to love another human being through you. You're now in recovery, yet there are many out there still burdened by shame and guilt, lost in their unworthiness, deep in regret, isolated, and barely existing in depression. These lost sheep have the calling of God on their lives, as you did, even during addiction. Shouldn't you have mercy on your fellow man, just as God had mercy on you?

They're starving for the unconditional love of their heavenly Father, and they are thirsty for his living waters. They need a helping hand to get back up out of the miry clay. As you extend your hand to help, you suddenly realize it is the hand of Jesus, reaching out through you.

God doesn't want anyone to perish. When the Father's compassion shines through you to another in the depth of their addiction, the foundation for your recovery strengthens.

Lord, I'm grateful you're always with me, to the end of time.
I pray I will have mercy on others, as you had on me. Amen.

MATTHEW 18:14, 33, 28:20; 2 PETER 3:9

Recover with the Father

Where is your mind traveling this day? You search and long for that perfect place of rest from the storms of past shame and regret; yet, a storm appearing on the horizon gets you off-track quickly. The enemy swoops in to invite you to choose his destination for promised relief, and in an instant, you find yourself budging into the front of the line for instant gratification. It's all a lie. The sunny day at the beach turns into an epic storm, with lightning and hailstones; you were tricked for the umpteenth time.

When you choose your spirit to be in charge, Jesus' lap to rest becomes much more inviting than anything your flesh can provide for relief. Gratitude increases; you praise and thank God for another day above ground.

The key for recovery is accountability; in fact, you can't recover alone by your own understanding. Submit to God and trust him with all you have. Your heavenly Father declares your worthiness. Jesus took your regret and shame, and the Holy Spirit strengthens and empowers you to have a great recovery.

Lord, I pray I will trust you with my recovery with all I've got. I'm grateful you deem me worthy to live a new life with you. Amen.

PROVERBS 3:5-6

Pray without Ceasing

When you pray without ceasing, it opens God's floodgates of blessing to you. Jesus is your rock and firm foundation, who leads and guides you. God would not allow the intense attacks that are coming at you, at this time, without sufficient grace to get through the difficulty of the test. When you acknowledge him with a grateful heart, he makes your crooked path straight. God equips and sustains you through what you're experiencing this day.

Thankfulness will override your fleshly desires to give up because the road seems so difficult. Gratitude chases self-pity right out the door! It's only when admitting to being poor that you escape from your false self and into that restful place of God's favor and blessing upon your life.

The truth is that you're not going through hell: that's where you've come from. By his grace, you will not quit, fail, or relapse when today's storm is blowing fiercely, because you'll be giving thanks in all circumstances.

Lord, I pray you will answer me when I call to you. I ask for relief from my distress, be merciful to me. Amen.

1 Thessalonians 5:16-18; Proverbs 3:5-6; Psalm 4:1

Give Everything to God

God invites you to bring everything on your plate to him: concerns, worries, frustrations, fear, and also your dreams. The light of Jesus' presence breathes life into your hopes and dreams, as he gently brings them into reality. When you step into God's grace to believe in the unseen, his eternal hope springs forth out of you.

God is bigger than fear. The great challenge is to embrace God's plan for you to prosper, grow in faith, and become certain of his spiritual principles. Only then can you willingly get out of his way and let him do for you what you always considered to be impossible.

Kick your ego and pride off the bus, get to the back, and enjoy God's perfect timing, schedule, leading, path, mercy, and love. God's plan will flourish in the midst of your battles and trials.

Lord, I pray to live by faith, not by sight. I pray to open up my closed windows, so your stuff can get in. Amen.

HEBREWS 11:1; 1 CORINTHIANS 5:7

Take Cover in God's Shelter

God's loving presence in your recovery provides a warmth and security you always dreamed of having. As you become more intimate with the one who saved you, trust in him grows. God promises to never forsake those who seek him.

Your intellect and reasoning can't comprehend the truth that God's tender mercies are available to you because he loves ruffians who admit their dire need of his grace. There is nothing you can do to qualify or earn it because it's his gift to you.

God will encourage and give you whatever you need to prepare you to let him love another into recovery through you. You must first release the storms of your life to God to enter the safety and refuge of his heavenly storm shelter. Jesus paid your debt to relieve all hindrances of legal charges the enemy would bring against you in the heavenly court. All debt is cancelled. You're now free to celebrate the freedom Jesus bought for you with his blood.

Lord, I pray to embrace you as my Father. I'm so grateful you'll be my guide even to the end. Amen.

PSALMS 9:10, 48:14

God's Lifeline

You'll experience moments when another step forward seems impossible, and you find yourself at the end of the rope with no hope. It's okay, that's a good thing: the end of the rope is where God begins. Even when the Father throws you his lifeline to grab, the stubborn flesh doesn't give up the pity party without a fight. It demands to continue rehearsing past hurts and resentment, and doesn't like to be told what to do.

While staring at God's lifeline, hanging onto the end of your rope, it's still a challenge to reach out, grab the lifeline, and release the stronghold. Through him who gives you strength, you can! It seems so simple, yet it's complicated in your mind.

With child-like faith, receive the refreshing breath of life, which delivers you. Jesus is able to save completely those who come to God through him, because he's always working on your behalf.

Lord, I pray I will grab your lifeline more quickly when I need it. I pray to not merely listen to your Word, but to do what it says. Amen.

PHILIPPIANS 4:13; HEBREWS 7:25; JAMES 1:22

You Have Access

God's will for you is not to quench the Spirit. Jesus brought you the good news of peace while you were far away from him, lost in depression. Through him, you now have access to the Father. It's essential to intentionally pursue recovery with the same intense energy you chased addiction. Your situations might not change, yet the Holy Spirit empowers you to change how to deal with the situation.

Sometimes you make it worse because you're holding on so tightly to control it, and you just can't leave it alone. You lose sleep over something you can do nothing about! When you release control over your recovery, you just passed the trust test.

Plant the seed, water it, and give the timetable to God. He's very capable of getting you where you need to be. Worry and anxiety ties God's hands. The miracle is that you're trusting God, and you're still standing.

Lord, I pray to give control of my recovery to you. I give you the glory that all things are from, and through, you. Amen.

EPHESIANS 2:17-18; ROMANS 11:36

Most Unlikely

Moses asked God to teach him everything he needed to know so he would find favor with God. God's response was simply that he would go with Moses and give him rest. God then revealed his glory in its full majestic splendor to Moses. It was so powerful, he had to cover Moses with his hand until he passed by. God continues to reveal his glory today.

Everything God does reveals his glory and majesty. God chose to reveal himself to you in order to bring himself glory. He sent his Son to bring you into recovery for the undeserved privilege of sharing in his glory.

When you stand firm for another day—sober, clean, and out of the casino—your actions bring great glory to the Father. His presence is with you this moment. Dare to believe this is your time.

Lord, it's truly amazing you chose to plant me in recovery to bring yourself glory. I pray to be an example of your glory. Amen.

EXODUS 33:13-22; PSALM 111:3; JOHN 11:40; ROMANS 5:2; JOHN 15:8

Content to Be Yourself

You must be on guard to not speak *about* your circumstances; rather, to speak *to* them. The Lord is a shield around you, your glory, and the one who holds your head high. God rescued you that you might glorify him, praise his name, and take up his rightful place to be at the center of your recovery. He set you in, and equips you with every good work to send you out. It seems a lot of work to become the person God wants you to be; that's a lie. It's no longer about you.

If you want to stand out, then step down, and become a servant. It's insanity to believe things will change with your ego and pride in control and your intellect working out every detail of your recovery in your brain.

You've been knocked down, beaten up, and left wondering if your life had any meaning. God promises your life will count if you are content with who you are. The intellectual in you asks what, why, and how? Step out of your reasoning to simply receive what God's Son did for you.

Lord, I pray I will speak to my circumstances, not about them. I pray to get out of my mind today and be content with who you say I am. Amen.

PSALMS 3:3, 50:15, 71:8; MATTHEW 23:11

God's Vision or Your Sight?

God's vision for you is a present-day revelation of his truth. There's a huge difference between vision and sight. You've believed what you see is going to be what you get. Sight is a function of the eyes, and you can only see so far. Vision, however, is what you see with your heart and imagination. God reveals his vision for you while in recovery, so you can see the unseen. It's a necessity to be connected to God's vision.

Connect with a mentor who has a vision of recovery for you. You need someone who has the vision to see the great potential in you. They'll remind you this is about God's vision and not your personal agenda. A man of understanding will draw greatness out of you from the deep waters of your heart.

God brought you into recovery and opened a door for you that no one can slam shut. Don't worry about being qualified. God works with what you have already. When your vision connects to a corporate vision, there will be much fruit.

Lord, I pray to see more with my heart than my eyes. I pray to be committed and faithful to the vision you gave me. Amen.

Proverbs 20:5, 29:18; Acts 16:9-10; Revelation 3:8

Stay Close to Jesus

As you begin to embrace the foundation God's constructing for you, a Spirit moment strikes at your inner core when you know, despite your past and present efforts, the kingdom of God is within you.

God gives you the full package, yet like a child, you need to learn how to walk in it so you can operate it effectively. Begin to identify feelings and emotions, so you learn to make good decisions during the pursuit of God's righteousness, peace, and joy. There might be bad things today, yet you can still have a great day, in him.

The greatest act of love was displayed at the cross of Christ, where he gave his life for you. You need to get this; the King left his heavenly throne to die for you. It's time to leave your self-righteous throne to gather around his. Anyone who serves Christ in this way is pleasing to God. Your recovery is dependent on becoming the hands and feet of Jesus—to be of service to others.

Lord, I pray to go deeper with you. I pray to stay close to where you are. Amen.

LUKE 17:21; ROMANS 14:17-18; JOHN 12:26, 15:13

Don't Leave before the Blessing

You're making solid progress anytime you say no to your selfish flesh. God honors and celebrates your effort even when you think it's a bit feeble. You need to check out why it's a challenge to do something good for someone. Often, it's related to believing the enemy's lie that you have nothing to offer. The flesh being lazy and selfish, with entitlement issues, keeps you locked into doing nothing. Busyness suggests strongly that you don't have enough time in the day to help someone else.

It's critical to work at your recovery with the same relentless effort you pursued the next fix. God tells it like it is: you were saved for a greater purpose than yourself. Half measures avail you nothing: get all in or be taken out. This is serious business.

When no one seems to notice your effort—there's no slap on the back or thanks—that's okay. God knows what you do. Don't get tired of doing what's good. Don't get discouraged and give up. Don't leave just before your blessing arrives.

Lord, I'm grateful you give me extra time when it's about you. I pray I will serve you when no one's looking. Amen.

GALATIANS 6:9

What He Did

The Word says to do to others what you would like them to do to you; it's a summary of all that's taught. You've probably heard the Golden Rule since a child, yet you didn't know it was directly from God. This is a huge challenge because when you were hurt, you hurt others. Under severe judgment, you judged, and self-condemnation produced finger-pointing and blame.

The enemy's path of self-destruction keeps rolling if you're around people who agree and co-sign your twisted thinking. In this dark dance of deflection of self, you rehearse your hurts, justify anger, and crucify those you've judged.

God demonstrated his great love for you by sending his Son to save you. If he did that for you, wouldn't you like to do something for him?

Lord, I pray I will do for you what you did for me and die to self. Thanks for completing the assignment the Father gave you, sacrificing your life for mine. Amen.

MATTHEW 7:12; ROMANS 5:6-8

Hope Opens the Door

There are three ways to commit suicide—to take your own life, allow yourself to die, or agree with the insanity of living without hope. The enemy has so delicately disguised living without hope that you can't recognize it. You think God's mad at you, and guilt from the pit of hell pronounces that you're unworthy of hope or any good thing. The one you truly deceive is yourself. Place your hope in the Lord and in his unfailing love and overflowing supply of salvation.

Hope encourages you to rest in Jesus' lap, and stay close to him as you walk into his calling. Don't be anxious; God isn't going to change his mind about you, and his gifts and call are irrevocable. You can stop arguing with yourself, and others, over insignificant and unimportant issues. There's sufficient grace available to break free from the distractions of chaos, lies, and deceit.

Welcome the child you're discovering within you, and get in touch with your child-like faith. It's the child in you who will welcome Jesus.

Lord, thanks for the gift of child-like faith. Hope in you replaces my thoughts of suicide. Amen.

PSALM 130:7; ROMANS 11:29; MATTHEW 18:5

It's Possible with God

It's critical to remember the moment you reached the destination of brokenness, standing knee deep in shame and unworthiness, beaten up, and laid low. King David had reached that moment when he prayed for God's mercy, unfailing love, and compassion.

God protected you for this opportunity to show off what he can do for you. The creator of the universe invites you to give him your nothingness, and get out of his way. What has been impossible for you is possible with God.

It doesn't matter how many times you've been hurt, or if you exist on the desolate island of depression. It's your turn to tap into his strength to get to where he desires you to be. God merely asks you to submit to him—to work your recovery his way for your benefit.

Lord, I pray to be a mountain-mover in my recovery, not a mountain-maker. I pray to remember my brokenness to know how far you've brought me. Amen.

PSALM 51:1; HEBREWS 11:3; LUKE 18:27

The Devil's Pawn Shop

God gives you authority to move out of the flesh and stop wagging your tongue, being critical, and planning every tiny detail of your next move. Let God handle your situation before it handles you. It's essential to remember your best thinking got you into some ugly places. Allow your nerves to quiet their twitching and not be overly sensitive. You're no longer a slave but a child of God, and everything he has now belongs to you. Your attitude is essential for God to work through you, to receive all he has for you.

Attitude determines your altitude. Is your altitude horizontal, stuck on the familiar and trying to get back what you lost? Or is it vertical, trusting God for the unfamiliar and what you're eager to give away? The Father has called you to live in freedom, to serve one another in love.

It's extremely critical for you to know God paid to redeem you out of the devil's pawn shop. If the Son sets you free, you'll be free to recover, free to love, free to serve, and free to help another be free.

Lord, I'm humbled your precious blood is already covering the situation I'm so worried and anxious about. I pray to intentionally receive your gift of freedom, with gratitude and thanksgiving. Amen.

GALATIANS 4:7, 5:13; 1 PETER 1:19; JOHN 8:32, 36

You Are Rich

Although pain is part of life, it's never easy to suffer. Christ knows of your afflictions and poverty, but you are rich! You're not to be afraid. The challenge during difficult times is to not lose focus on the prize or become twisted by what others say or do. The danger is to get drawn into the chaos and confusion. As the battle heats up, the first reaction is to deal with what's happening out of emotion. Seek God's guidance and infinite mercy for his help.

Your busy mind is not a good rudder for your recovery ship. You end up minimizing and making excuses, even when isolated and wondering why you're having a bad day. Don't beat yourself up! The enemy tricked you to operate in the lie that it's all up to you.

Ask God for wisdom, and it will be given to you. In him, you can have a good day, in spite of bad things happening.

Lord, I pray to stand fast during adversity knowing that you know. I pray to ask for wisdom a bit quicker than I normally do. Amen.

REVELATION 2:9; MATTHEW 16:8; JAMES 1:5

No Middle Ground

Just as you get physical check-ups, spiritual check-ups are also needed. There's no middle ground with recovery. You're either seeking your new life with expectancy, and walking God's path; or drifting along hoping for mainline blessing with sideline commitment, and walking your path. Are your actions revealing growth?

If you don't have regular spiritual check-ups, you'll end up in the enemy's emergency room, which is not a good place to be. Your only hope is to get the living Word in you. If you don't know who Jesus is, the storms and tsunamis of life will take you out.

God asks you to keep his words and store up his commands within you, in order that you might live. Some moms used to tie strings on their kids' fingers to remind them about something important. Ask God for his string to remind you.

Lord, I pray to protect and guard your teachings within me. I pray for courage to have regular, spiritual check-ups. Amen.

2 CORINTHIANS 13:5; PROVERBS 1:7

Unlikely Mentors

Unworthiness and anxiety gets us to stumble over the remnant of insecurity. That's when it's time to visit some of your most powerful spiritual mentors. They're not in recovery, they haven't been in treatment or experienced a relapse, they don't criticize, shame, or blame, and they forgive immediately with a hug. They have the capacity for an ocean of unconditional love, their smile of joy lights up an auditorium, and trust is freely given.

Children. They show the fullness of God living in a human body. Oh yes, we can act childish, in an instant. A tiny pebble on the huge battlefield of the mind gets us distracted. Throw a hissy-fit to get attention? Absolutely! Whine to get what we want? Yes! Play with a toy for two minutes and go to the next? Always! That's okay.

Connect your child-like faith with a child, and play. Receive God's pure love through them. For a moment, all else falls away.

Lord, I pray for protection of the children in my life. I pray each gets to know you as I experience you. Thanks for the gift of child-like faith. Amen.

COLOSSIANS 2:9

Embrace the Fruit

Your flesh absolutely abhors bringing anything into the light. It detests instruction, counsel, and truth, and keeps secrets with lies and deceit. It will never accept blame or responsibility. *I know what I'm doing! Don't tell me what to do! I know what's best!* These are three simple examples of pride speaking through your lips. It's essential to not rely on your own thinking. Without godly counsel, there will be wrong choices that are dangerous.

The world says you're weak when admitting your humanness. Jesus promises that when you admit you're weak, he makes you strong. The ultimate destroyer is out to twist you into trading the Holy Spirit's fruit in your life for your sinful nature.

The addict in you is capable of mass destruction. Let Jesus strengthen you to embrace the fruit of the Holy Spirit and live in freedom, one day at a time.

Lord, I pray I will keep telling on myself. I pray to choose the fruit of the Holy Spirit today and be a testimony of God's grace. Amen.

GALATIANS 5:22-23, 19-21

A Loyal and Trusted Friend

Marines, Special Forces, Green Berets, Delta Teams, Rangers, and others totally focus on their mission, their buddy, and those in their unit. A friend is always loyal, and a brother is born to help in time of need: this is displayed in the courageous act that no one is left behind.

Would you die for a friend? Soldiers will die to bring a fallen buddy back to their family. Would you die for someone already dead? That's exactly what Jesus did. He gave his life, shedding his precious blood for you while you were dead in sin.

You're now a soldier for Christ and on the battlefield against an enemy who's out to steal, kill, and destroy you. Are you willing to die to yourself, and for God, your Commander-in-Chief?

Lord, I pray I will follow your command: to love others as you have loved me. I pray to fight for those still suffering. Amen.

JOHN 10:10, 15:12-13

Not too Hard

Be okay with your efforts of doing the best you can. It's okay to *want to* give up; however, it's not okay to *actually* give up. Don't lose heart; God never gives you more than you can handle. The enemy is the liar who says you're not doing enough, you're always falling short, and others are to blame for your problems. Soon, you're offended by every small thing and have hundreds of excuses and reasons why life is too hard.

Life is truly hard when on a prison chain-gang, using a fifty-pound sledgehammer, breaking rock from morning light to dark, on a hot, humid day. Life was hard when feeding your addiction, abused and tortured by the enemy of your soul, and believing an addict was all you'd ever be.

Consider this day a walk in the park as you're above ground, breathing, and out of your self-made prison. God invites you to follow his commands, which are not too difficult for you to understand, or perform. Recovery only becomes too hard when you're in control of it.

Lord, give me happiness, for my life depends on you. I pray for gratitude when thinking life is too hard. Amen.

GALATIANS 6:9; DEUTERONOMY 30:11; PSALM 86:3-4

Do What You Don't Feel like Doing

To be passive is to do nothing. When you confront your false self and admit you don't do anything, you begin to do something about your recovery. You've lived in the world of doing what you feel like doing. The enemy twisted you to do nothing except pursue your addiction with every ounce of strength in your body, even when you didn't feel like it.

It's critical to do what the enemy and flesh don't want you to do. A great start is to seek the kingdom of God; it will save your life. You begin to do things you don't feel like, so you can do things you want and need to do. In recovery, you begin participating by becoming more intentional on what needs to be done. You're more deliberate.

Sidestep the quicksand of "I don't feel like it" to embrace "I'm going to do it anyway," and pursue recovery as you did your addiction.

Lord, I pray I will do what I don't feel like doing. I pray to know more deeply what you want me to do. Amen.

MATTHEW 6:33; EPHESIANS 5:17

Jesus Wept

Two powerful words describe the profound empathy Jesus has for you when experiencing grief and sorrow at the loss of a loved one. When Jesus saw Mary weeping for her brother, Lazarus, and those with her also weeping, he was deeply moved in spirit and troubled. He wept.

Addiction has taken its toll upon the lives of ruffians who medicate their pain with drugs, alcohol, and gambling. Some are swept out of recovery never to be heard from again, others relapse and fight to get back on track, and many have died of overdose and suicide.

For those who have endured heartfelt grief and pain because of depression, loss of relationship, a shattered family, a dear one whose location is unknown, a sudden heart attack, traumatic accident, or death by suicide or overdose—Jesus weeps with you. He meets you right where you are. When ravaged by grief, take comfort in God's promise of protection and relief. He wipes away all your tears.

Lord, I pray for a tender heart to weep with those who are grieving. I pray to honor the legacy of those who died by overdose by loving another addict into recovery. Amen.

JOHN 11:33-35; REVELATION 7:17

Become a Giver

You want to do everything, to the best of your ability, to finish the course God set for you with joy. Addiction set itself up above all things in your life, and would constantly nag you to feed it. Jesus came to express his radical gospel with the invitation to follow him.

You've been looking for love in all the wrong places. The only measurement of your life with meaning and purpose rests in the one who calls you to rest in him. The reflection of God's grace through you is where fulfillment awaits. You already know seeking recognition, status, and approval from others has left you empty, walking on eggshells, and unfulfilled.

Choices await you on a daily basis: be selfless or selfish, give or take, respect or disrespect, be wise or foolish, tell the truth or lie, encourage or discourage, pardon or accuse, speak words of life or death. Jesus throws a curve ball at your flesh when he says it's better to give than receive.

Lord, I pray for strength to take less and give more. I pray for courage to speak words of life over myself and others, no matter the situation. Amen.

ACTS 20:24, 35; LUKE 9:23

Stay or Go

Many enter treatment with tears of gratitude, and the most famous statement of all—I'll never use again; I'll never go back! A month later, it's all changed; recovery is miserable, I can do this alone, and I'm using again!

Recovery is serious business: it's life or death. It's sad to witness a beloved of Jesus work a strong recovery, leave before ready, and fall down the slippery slope they swore they would stay away from. If lazy in recovery, you'll get put back to work in a relapse.

This isn't about yesterday's medallion, it's about today: a gift from God. You're given another opportunity to show his love by respecting others, especially yourself. Your new heart will love another into recovery, and your new Spirit will encourage the newcomer to stay.

Lord, I pray protection over those who go back into chaos and addiction. I praise you with an upright heart as I learn about you. Amen.

EZEKIEL 36:26; PSALM 119:7

Commitment, Effort, Persistence

You've got to know where you've been to have a sense of where you're going. With God, your destination is secure, yet the journey to get there is dependent on being found faithful. You begin by commitment to stop using your drug of choice, effort to do whatever is needed, and being persistent to get some time in recovery. God's able to guard you during this challenging transition, when entrusting your recovery to him.

Endure hardship as a good soldier of Christ Jesus. It's not *if* hardship comes, it's *when* hardship comes. God allowed the enemy to train you in the area of going all in for something. You have it in you to pursue recovery with the same commitment, effort, and persistence you tracked down drugs, sought alcohol, or continued to gamble.

Think, meditate, and pray about this—the Lord will give you insight and understanding in this area. God desires to prepare and increase the gift already in you, so that you might believe recovery is for you.

Lord, I pray I get to know your Word. I pray my recovery doesn't become a stagnant pond; but rather, a pond stirred up with your living water flowing through it to others. Amen.

1 TIMOTHY 1:13; 2 TIMOTHY 2:3, 7

Trials Develop Character

Trials come to reveal where you're at in recovery. This is character development time. The enemy comes to distract you from allowing God's process to continue, while your flesh responds by complaining, blaming, and shaming. Let trouble and tough times be an opportunity. When your faith is tested, endurance has a chance to grow. God promises to bless those who hang in there, in spite of intense pressure to give up.

It's critical to know God's already taken care of whatever trials and sorrows you're going through. You can claim the peace of Christ to be with you during the struggle that comes. God's peace allows you not to get entangled with issues, legal consequences, or working so hard to get back what you lost.

You already tried to be in control of all your stuff. How did that work out? Trust God to take care of what you're tripping on; he's already working on your behalf.

I pray to stay out of your way when working on my stuff. I pray to endure, to be blessed with more character. Amen.

JAMES 1:2-4, 12; JOHN 16:33

Activate Your Recovery

When you realize that God is teaching you to trust him, it's a bit overwhelming. Did you ever think, in your wildest dreams, you were even worthy of being taught, personally, by the God who created all things? Just as a squirrel works so diligently to hide and store the food it needs during the winter months, God is depositing his Word in you so you can withdraw from his supply whatever you need for each day. He knows exactly what to put in you to get what he wants out of you.

It's only when you get connected that you get the supply you need. It's essential to release what you don't need, so he can give you more. Focus all your energy on forgetting the past and looking forward to what lies ahead.

Your hope is now in Christ. Embrace his forgiveness. The Word of God is alive and full of power. It will convince you of the differences between God and the enemy. Get into the Word, and allow it to activate your recovery.

PROVERBS 22:19; PHILIPPIANS 3:13; HEBREWS 4:12

Get Your Inside Put Right

In spite of what's going on with your situation and circumstance, God says you're okay. You're blessed when you get your inside world—your mind and heart—put right. It's only then you can see God in the outside world. The simplicity of your new life is based upon knowing you're no longer alone, and connecting to others in recovery for accountability and support.

As confusion, chaos, worry, and fear rise from the pit of hell, God's Spirit empowers you to stand firm in the faith. Others in recovery are going through the same kind of suffering. God doesn't just call you; he fully equips you, and brings you into the place of undeserved privilege where you now stand.

You can look forward to sharing God's glory with confidence and joy. If you aren't confident and joyful for what you have, why would God give you more? God's able to accomplish more through you than you could ever ask, or dream of.

Lord, I pray to get my inside put right, to see you in the outside. I'm grateful for my calling and for your glory. Amen.

MATTHEW 5:8; 1 PETER 5:8-9; ROMANS 5:1-2; EPHESIANS 3:20

Actions Speak Louder

Here's a phrase you've heard many times: actions speak louder than words. There's a difference between being told to do something, and choosing to do something. The truth is you have to do some things for your recovery, and it's only your actions that will activate the construction of a firm foundation. Self-pity says, "Oh darn, I have to," while gratitude declares, "Alleluia, I get to." Without action, faith is dead!

You declare his glory all day long by your actions because your actions might be the only Bible people see. When someone sees you, do they see Jesus? If someone could spy on you while you were in your house alone, would they see Jesus?

Actions are powerful and reveal excuses, reasons, and justifications. Who set you free for action? Jesus paid your debt, wiped off your filthy slate with his blood, and prepared an eternal mansion for you. His action set you free for your faith and action to work together.

Lord, I'm thankful there's a season and a time under heaven for action. I pray to stop making excuses for not doing anything, and be empowered by your action at the cross to do something. Amen.

JAMES 2:17, 22; ECCLESIASTES 3:1

Offer Yourself to God

The very act of offering your body as a living sacrifice is your spiritual worship to the one who created you. When you acknowledge God's presence in your new life in recovery, it's pleasing to him. Jesus' earthly ministry appeared to be a failure and his life ineffective as he was arrested, tortured, pronounced guilty, and murdered on the cross. Yet, his cry of compassion and great love for you resounded throughout the universe with the simple words, "I love you, in spite of all you've done."

As he offered himself for you, he is requesting you to offer yourself for him. There is absolutely no more precious act of worship from you than to intentionally become the hands and feet of Jesus. Your flesh demands to be in charge and is rebellious to God's teaching. The Holy Spirit is comforting, encouraging, and strengthens you to stand your ground and not back down.

God desires intimacy with you and meets you where you are. In a reckless display of faith, dare to crucify your egotistical self on the cross, to become his disciple by taking up your cross daily and following him.

Lord, I pray to become holy and pleasing to you. I pray to receive your love to the fullest. Amen.

ROMANS 12:1; LUKE 9:23

No Longer Condemned

When you feel condemnation and shame, it's because you're believing the lie of the enemy and walking according to the flesh. In fact, the entire human race is on death row because of sin. Thank God, Jesus stepped in to represent you in the heavenly court, gave himself as a sacrifice for your sins, and had his Father pronounce you "not guilty."

The mission of the enemy of your soul is to undermine the greatest act of love ever displayed in the universe. The devil wants to twist you into thinking what God did and what Jesus did was not enough! When you allow God's Spirit to join with your spirit, he affirms that you're chosen to be his child. If God is for you, who can ever be against you? You've been to hell and back. It's your turn to rest in your heavenly Father's embrace.

Lord, I pray to trust that what you did for me broke my addiction. I pray to believe, by faith, I'm now one of your kids. Amen.

ROMANS 8:1-3, 8:16, 31

God Will Never Leave You

The key for recovery is to patiently endure testing and temptation, and stay long enough to receive your blessings and promises. Your tests become your testimony, and the seed planted within you, before birth, will bear fruit. You've tried for years, but character defects kept you locked in the revolving door of detox, treatment, jail, and relapse. There's stuff in you that absolutely needs to be removed to stop this chaos and insanity, which you cannot do yourself.

God's been patiently waiting for you to need him and will remove anything you give him. Can you be patient with the one who was patient with you? You did not choose God; He chose you. Trust him to remove the imperfections that existed before ever medicating your pain and shame.

God is with you, protects you, and will not leave you until he gives you everything promised. God's not slow about these promises; he's patient for your sake, until you can handle his blessings. God's not dead, and is training you to receive what he has for you. Don't leave before the blessing!

Lord, I pray for the courage to participate with you in my recovery. I pray to remain humble, so I'm not humiliated. Amen.

JAMES 1:2; 2 PETER 3:15; JOHN 15:16; GENESIS 28:15

Faith, Freely Given

God changed Abram's name to Abraham because of his great faith in absolutely believing in the God who brings into existence what didn't exist before. Abraham was completely convinced God could do anything he promised.

This call to faith is freely given to you. Trust God's already working on your behalf. You're no longer on a ship tossed about during a violent storm, with no hope. God desires that you allow him to do for you what you couldn't do for yourself. You've tried everything else; you might as well try God.

There will be worries, frustrations, fear, and guilt coming at you; it just means you're on the right track. God can turn the worst of the worst into the best of the best. How much faith, this day, is needed? Just a tiny mustard seed of faith, vibrant and growing, is all that's needed to say to any mountain standing before you, "Move from here to there," and it would move. Relax and chill a bit, as your faith allows you to know recovery is for you.

I pray to claim God's promise for my recovery, by faith like Abraham. I pray my faith in God continues to grow so my recovery grows. Amen.

ROMANS 4:21, 17; MATTHEW 17:20

People of Purpose

God's purpose for you is not to be an addict, depressed, isolated or miserable. The truth says you have one purpose—to worship God forever. God desires your time, talent, and tithe. In the past, you pursued anything that would fill the emptiness that only God could fill. God's great love for you always protects, trusts, hopes, and perseveres. It's essential to grasp that the choices made today can be a blessing for you, your children and their children. The rest of your life can be the best of your life.

You learn the principle of purpose for your life by being around people of purpose to observe their deeds, love, faith, service, and perseverance. Measure yourself, and yet, know it's not easy to know how you're doing in the midst of a trial or storm.

Reach out to the people of purpose you've been watching. As his living water begins flowing in and through you to others, stick and stay to allow perseverance to finish its work.

I pray I will learn from those who have purpose. I pray to ask others what they see in me. Amen.

JEREMIAH 33:3; 1 CORINTHIANS 13:6-7; REVELATION 2:19; JAMES 1:4

What Holds You Back

Addicts protect the secret little domains of control and the need to express opinions on just about everything. An emotional response can be used to reinforce what you're already going to do. Like a master architect, you move people into their places, manipulate an argument until you can blame someone, and head off to the races under your own power, resentful and closed-minded. Your only hope is to go boldly to the throne and bring to the light the enemy stronghold in your life.

God's love melts the fear of letting go. Lost courage is found, night fright becomes peaceful rest, and procrastination is replaced by action. Impossible? Your fears for today, worries about tomorrow, and even the powers of hell can't keep God's love away. He relentlessly pursued you by sending his only Son to die, so that you might live.

Love has no room for fear. Fear always has to do with punishment, and is washed away by the Father's living Word.

Lord, I pray to remain in you, so your Word remains in me.
I pray your love will save me from myself. Amen.

ROMANS 8:37-39; 1 JOHN 4:10; JOHN 4:18

The Joy of God's Presence

There will be days when the strain of your recovery journey seems endless. You walk with heavy legs and your feet hurt. Anxiety comes when you can't seem to hit the reset button of joy. As the enemy pours more kerosene on the anxiety bonfire, the Holy Spirit's still, quiet voice whispers, "Be always full of joy in the Lord—rejoice!" It is such a gift you are to search for it as if it were a hidden treasure. God wants you to have it, and he will guide you to it.

Soon, without great effort, you stumble upon the hidden treasure identified by his Spirit in you. God's still around listening, caring, and loving you. As the Father lifts you into his lap, he reassures you to stand firm to the end and trust him. Enjoy those moments in his special place, laughing and giggling.

Rejoice that you survived the day's opposition and received your Father's extravagant love and compassion. Don't give up.

God, I ask for grace to praise you when I'm stuck and don't want to. I thank you for making me glad with the joy of your presence. Amen.

PHILIPPIANS 4:4; MATTHEW 24:13; PSALM 21:6

Without Love, You Have Nothing

Your flesh is stubborn, hostile, and demands physical proof of God. It doesn't grasp spiritual teachings, and simply rejects that God approves and loves you. As you begin to know you're worthy to receive the Father's love, it penetrates deeply into your innermost parts. Without love, you have nothing.

The devil is the father of lies, a murderer from the beginning, who has no truth in him. He is out to distract, disrupt, confuse, and distort your efforts in recovery. The enemy presents a counterfeit for every blessing God has already prepared for you. The liar wants you to agree that because of your past, you're a loser and worthy of only punishment and death.

Jesus says he's in you and you're in him, and gives you the same glory his Father gave him. This is for you to know, without reservation, that there's nothing you can ever do for God to love you more, or for him to love you less.

Lord, I pray to be watchful and pray. Thanks for not giving up on me. Amen.

MARK 14:38; MATTHEW 22:37; JOHN 8:44, 17:21-23

A Good Fall

God shows mercy and compassion to anyone he chooses, and he chose you for recovery. There will be opposition to living a life free from addiction, because the world's values are not God's values. It's an extremely dangerous game to attempt recovery while one foot remains in the world.

Intellect and reasoning demand to be in control of decisions concerning your present and future. When you stumble, the enemy usually gets credit for derailing your recovery, but the rock you sometimes stumble over is Jesus.

You stumble when conforming to the world's values. It could be a good thing; you might just stumble into humility, fall into his peace, or even blunder into obedience to the one who saved you.

Lord, I pray to raise my white flag of surrender. I pray to stumble and fall into you. Amen.

ROMANS 9:15, 33

Close Down Your Dungeon

In the past, when shame, disgrace, regret, and pain became too much to endure, you medicated with whatever was available. You constructed what you thought was a safe place, deep within yourself, to run and hide. What you thought a safe shelter, the enemy tweaked into a dungeon. You became familiar with the dark underground prison, and escaped only by the grace of God. When hopeless, powerless, and homeless, with no place to turn, God brought you to your senses and saved you from the devil's trap.

In recovery, you need to ask God to totally remove the dungeon, so it's no longer available for use. The enemy attempts to twist and trick you to use it to torture those who hurt you deeply. Ask the Holy Spirit to remove the submerged, subterranean place of betrayal, hate, and offense as far as the east is from the west.

Ask him to refill the once bottomless, underground chamber of mental, spiritual, and physical suffering with his goodness.

Lord, I know you heard my prayer and closed my dungeon, forever. I pray I will forgive those who betrayed and hurt me deeply. Amen.

1 CORINTHIANS 15:33; GALATIANS 5:22-23

The King Chose You

At meetings, you often hear, "I chose God." Do you seriously believe you had the power to choose God when at your darkest moment, broken, flat on your face, and reduced to nothing? No one was there for you, and you couldn't even find a shoulder to cry on.

God chose to lift you from the darkness at the very moment you were the least deserving and most undesirable, just to reveal his eternal, unconditional love for you.

Jesus made a lot of choices for you. Without the choices made by your Lord and Savior, you wouldn't have a choice. Choose today whom you will serve. It's not about what God's going to do, because he's doing it. It's always about what you'll do. Choose to serve the one who chose you.

Lord, I praise you for choosing me in spite of my past. I pray for courage to go and bear fruit, to honor you. Amen.

PSALM 69:20; JOHN 15:16; JOSHUA 24:15

Rise Up and Help Me

Whatever situation you're facing today—whether a circumstance pounding on the door, or doomsday seems to be approaching—the thought of medicating again can be very real. Take a deep breath, and pray. The Father's unconditional love reaches down from his Son's cross to declare you're worthy, washed clean, and good to go, regardless of what you think or feel. He's bigger than any circumstance or depression.

It's a challenge when despair, regret, depression, abuse, guilt, shame, condemnation, and resentment come messing around in the battlefield of your mind. The simplicity of God's message speaks volumes.

Separate yourself from what's pulling you away from peace, to find a place where peace can pull you in. The Word of God lasts forever. Get into the living Word to know God's there for you.

Lord, I pray to turn to you first when feeling low. I'm grateful the power of your Word can quiet my mind. Amen.

PSALM 44:25-26; ISAIAH 40:8

God Chooses the Least Likely

The carpenter from Nazareth was a great teacher by his actions and example. Jesus knew who he was and he permitted nothing, and no one, to stand in the way of being himself. He laughed, wept, loved, and remained true to his Father—seeking only to please him. He had no shame, yet took your shame upon himself and cleansed you with his precious blood.

Jesus loved to be around ruffians. He chose the least likely to show off through them and because he desires relationship with them. Check out Jesus' chosen followers: a hated tax collector, one who denied him three times, one who completely betrayed him, and some who were overcome by fear after he was laid in the tomb.

All were powerless until the Holy Spirit's fire came on them, transforming them into world changers. God has no favorites. Jesus will do for you what he did for them. They were the least likely. Ask for his power to reveal his glory through you.

Lord, I'm but a speck without your love and your advocacy. I pray I will be available for your calling to serve. Amen.

LUKE 24:28-35; ROMANS 2:11

You Are a Champion

The enemy's spiritual roadblocks are set up to hinder your effectiveness and distract you with deceit, irritation, and offense. The struggle in your mind is much like a heavy-weight boxing match between Jesus, the Champion, and Satan, the pretender contender. The pretender throws the punch of sadness, the Messiah counters with joy. The bully punches with anger, and Jesus fights back with kindness. The antagonist hits with anxiety and worry, the healer responds with patience and peace. The assailant lays down temptation, and the Lord of Lords quickly strikes back with faithfulness. The knock-out punch was Jesus' resurrection. Jesus takes off his gloves, and the match is over!

Your excuses for running to the pretender's corner lessen as you embrace being the beloved of Jesus, who accepts you as you are. You linger in his presence a bit longer than last week. As you become more real with yourself, and others, it's critical to reveal the little foxes you think are insignificant. They can knock you out of being the champion Jesus says you are.

Lord, I'm grateful for your victory in the boxing ring. Help me to stay in your corner for the remainder of the fight. Amen.

EPHESIANS 5:8; JOHN 1:4-5

Compassion and Comfort

You need to get this! You've been delivered from the slimy pit, out of the mud and mire. God set your feet on a rock and gave you a firm place to stand. You're now strategically positioned to receive God's revelation of his promises which are waiting to burst forth.

There are no self-help books, brilliant philosophy, great ideas, or any power point to get you to where you desire to be. You've tried everything to no avail, yet because of his love for you, God put you into position to check out what he has for you.

The Father who comforted you in all your troubles wants you to help comfort others. You can't keep his compassion and comfort to yourself. You're being transformed from celebrating what you did, to rejoicing in what he will do through you.

Lord, I pray I will be available for others, because you are there for me. I pray I will take very seriously what you have for me. Amen.

PSALM 40:2; 2 CORINTHIANS 1:3-4

The Blessing in Serving

Your dedication prayer for your recovery is to serve as Jesus served. Serving others is critical, and he places a protective covering over you when your pride and ego get kicked to the back of the bus. It's critical to give up your self-created throne—the world of you! God answers your prayers according to the way you live and what's in your heart.

Jesus, God in the flesh, provides the example to follow. The Messiah knelt before his disciples to wash their dirty feet, to show them the full extent of his love. Jesus' action of service teaches you how essential it is to become a servant to others. This was Jesus last night with the disciples and he was preparing them for their mission—to serve God, each other, and especially the people who were going to hear the precious, priceless message of salvation.

Now that you know these things, you will be blessed if you do them. Get out of yourself and do it.

Lord, I pray I will follow your example, even when I don't want to. Thanks for guarding and rescuing me when I reverently fear you. Amen.

1 KINGS 8:39; JOHN 13:1-17; PSALM 34:7

Fight for Quiet Time

Practice each day moments of being silent during prayer and devotions to honor God. Only then is it possible to have an intimate togetherness with the one who speaks with a soft, calm voice, and actually hear him. This can be quite a task, as busyness and distractions interrupt quiet time in an instant. When you're reading the words of truth, listen very carefully, or you may drift away. You need to be intentional to focus on the principles God desires you to learn.

It's a challenge to listen to the details of the Father's instruction or encouragement. Your corrupt nature is opposed to your spiritual nature and does not grasp spiritual teachings, is hostile to God, and has a limited perspective. That's why it's extremely important to cherish the moments you spend resting in Jesus' lap, hearing his heartbeat. He nurtures you to feed the spirit within you, causing the flesh to starve.

When you seek him with a humble heart, Jesus will be with you; yet, it's in the stillness of quiet moments he can remain.

Lord, I pray for discipline to seek you when waking up. I pray to listen more intently to the Holy Spirit. Amen.

PSALM 46:10; HEBREWS 2:1; GALATIANS 5:17

You're Okay

When some nights seem darker than others, violent storms and shadow figures invade dreams. Fear sweeps about like a floating spider web in the breeze, and as you suddenly awake, your heartbeat is faster and you're sweating.

It can be intensely real. You look forward to the first light of the new day, and pray. And rest and sleep comes again. It's important to pray for wisdom to know the truth about what you go through; God's priceless gift of wisdom will assure you that you're okay.

Be encouraged; nightmares and dreams of using will show up, but they will come less and less as you get some time in recovery. Tell someone about it as it lessens your fear and anxious thoughts. Your true rest can only be found in Jesus. Trust that God will keep you in perfect peace with the same intensity you used to trust your drug dealer, bartender, or casino dealer to relieve your pain. You've got it in you!

Lord, I pray to not let my heart be troubled or be afraid. I take heart because you've overcome the world. Amen.

PSALM 143:8; JOHN 14:27, 16:33

Guidance and Counsel

A wise man has great power, and knowledge increases your strength. While standing knee deep in unworthiness, you need guidance to wage the war to recovery, and many advisors to claim victory. It doesn't matter how much you've been hurt, or all the months you've barely existed in depression. It's your turn to ask for his strength when obstacles come your way. Once you were a master manipulator and control freak; why in recovery are you weak and ineffective? Rise out of your slumber; God's glory rises to shine on you.

The Father asks you to submit and allow him to work out your circumstances. The Son of Man came to seek you and save you when you were lost. When you grumble and complain, your ungrateful self is in control again. Let go and let God work out your steps for his glory.

If you're not fighting for recovery, your flesh will demand to get high. If you're not walking in God's truth, you're listening to the devil's lie. To fight the good fight against the enemy and your sinful nature, you need guidance and advice.

Lord, I pray to receive the truth that sets me free, and reject the devil's lies that make slavery seem so attractive at times. Amen.

PROVERBS 24:5-6; ISAIAH 60:1; LUKE 19:10; JOHN 8:32

Free, Indeed

God gave his life as a ransom for you to have authority over your flesh. The Holy Spirit empowers you to enjoy the peace when your nerves quiet their twitching. You're no longer a slave but one of God's children. Everything he has belongs to you.

Your flesh demands physical proof, is prideful, and hates to be told what to do. When God whispers not to do anything because he's got it, your flesh throws a hissy-fit. Let God handle the situation, or the situation will handle you.

Accept that you now belong to him and have become a new person. Your new life has begun. You glorify God when submitting to his authority, knowing Jesus' blood is already covering the situation you've been trying to control for years.

Lord, I pray to grasp that if you set me free, I'm indeed free, regardless of the enemy telling me I'm not. Amen.

MARK 10:45; GALATIANS 4:7, 5:13; 2 CORINTHIANS 5:17

For His Glory

You've always had a tendency not to let others into your space, living in fear of relationships because of experiences in your past. In fact, many fall into the enemy's trap of keeping the very people who speak words of life over them, away from them. Your false self was caught up in the game of looking good, regardless of how bad you felt. You believed you were the reflection you saw in the enemy's mirror. Your compassionate Father declares you to be a champion. He believes in you and saved you for his glory.

This isn't about your performance; it's about Jesus' performance and what he already did for you. Your heavenly Father reveals himself through his Son to show you what love looks and feels like. Jesus invites you to accept the Father's love through him, so the glorious light of the Gospel message breaks through the darkness.

God's tender mercies allow you to look in his mirror to see how he sees you, and empowers you to embrace the tenderness of the new relationships he gives you, in his name.

Lord, I pray I will see myself as you see me. I pray to know the glorious light of the gospel message is for me. Amen.

JOHN 10:30, 15:8, 17:10

Get to Know God

Recovery is not just for those in addiction, it's for all who call themselves Christians. It's a continual, daily spiritual conversion and all have failed miserably a number of times. Most of the failures to act on the Word of God are traced to ignorance, distraction, or lack of knowledge of who God truly is.

You can know of God, but only in an intimate relationship do you get to know him and walk with him. You don't know who your heavenly Father is if you're only spending a short time with him on Sundays. Don't get offended; the truth is Jesus upset the Pharisee's religious applecart, and he is out to upset yours.

Do you know you've been crucified with Christ and he now lives in you? Cast aside your Pharisee robe and grab your cross.

Lord, I pray you rise up and help me; redeem me because of your unfailing love. I pray to know you more intimately. Amen.

MATTHEW 10:38; GALATIANS 2:20; PSALM 44:26

Smell like Smoke

You have been chosen and called from where you were, for his greater purpose, so you may believe and know God. The daily miracle you sometimes forget is you're out of prison, alive, and breathing. As God opens eyes that were blind, he frees and releases you from prison and darkness.

It's a huge challenge to walk a new, unfamiliar path. The enemy suggests backsliding into what's familiar. The temptation can get intensely hot, as a furnace, yet God promises you won't get burned when walking through the fire of testing.

Shadrach, Meshach, and Abednego refused to worship the king's god and were thrown into a blazing furnace. They said the God whom they serve was able to save them from the blazing furnace. Even if he didn't, they said they would never serve or worship the king's god. They were thrown into the blazing furnace and delivered by an angel. When they came out, no hair on their heads was singed, clothing wasn't scorched, and they didn't even smell like smoke. Trust that God can walk with you through any intense, hot trial.

Lord, I pray I will stand for you whatever the consequence. I pray to follow you, no matter where you take me. Amen.

ISAIAH 42:7, 43:2, 10; DANIEL 3

Stay Connected

After searching for love in all the wrong places, it's a daunting task to receive the warmth and security of God's loving presence. In recovery, you confront your past relationships and admit most of them failed because you were in them. Your greatest gift of love is to embrace what true love has already done—Jesus left his heavenly throne for you. God Almighty desires an intimate togetherness with you regardless of what you've done.

Hang out with the one who loves you, and get to know his truth. Your flesh screams to be in control and pursue only that which you can see and touch. God invites you to fix your eyes on what is unseen. It's your season to stop pursuing what's temporary and seek what's eternal.

Only God provides refuge and shelter during this journey, and he is always working for your common good. God promises peace to his people and empowers you to say no to the false promises, chaos, and insanity of the enemy.

Lord, I pray to remain connected to your people so I won't have to go back to chaos and insanity. I'm grateful you always deliver me. Amen.

2 CORINTHIANS 4:18; PSALM 85:8

Foolish and Weak

You've tried everything your way and under your own power, searching for peace and a safe place to rest. This isn't about being good, doing good, and saying the right words. It's all about accepting what you can't do for yourself and trusting what God can do for you.

You're encouraged and uplifted when you're willing to know a power greater than yourself laid it all on the line for you. The message of the cross is foolish to those perishing, but to you it's powerful.

In the past, when sinking into utter despair from shame, you got high, drank, or gambled. It's essential to let go and let God, because you can't figure this out in the battlefield of your mind. Embracing the crucified Christ can't be done in the busyness between your ears. In the flesh, it sounds foolish. Truth declares that the foolishness of God is wiser than man's wisdom, and the weakness of God is stronger than man's strength. You will have a great day if you receive the foolishness and the weakness of God to give you wisdom and strength.

Lord, I pray to take your foolishness and weakness over my wisdom and strength one day at a time. Thanks for your wisdom to know my thinking can take me to some ugly places. Amen.

1 CORINTHIANS 1:18, 23-25

A Misnomer

The spirit of perfectionism is a lie from the pit. God alone is perfect. You aren't perfect, and you can never be perfect. Let it go!

A famous orchestra conductor takes his baton, raises both arms high, and whips the baton in a wild, unique double-8 circle. The music begins with each note being held accountable under the strict code of the conductor's musical ear. However, an incorrect note flowed upon his senses, then another, soon a lazy sliding note, and a floating note. The conductor began sweating profusely and placed the baton on the podium stand, feeling like a failure.

The ninety-three musicians stopped playing as a deafening silence came upon the hall. The conductor took a handkerchief out of his coat pocket to wipe his brow, and as the cloth was lifted, a violin began to play; the cloth lowered and brought more instruments into play. As the conductor loosened his necktie still holding the handkerchief, all the instruments entered into a sacred moment of harmonious melody.

Brilliance came forth from the wild movements of an off-white hanky, and perfectionism was kicked out the door.

Lord, I pray to put down the baton of perfectionism for my recovery. I pray to wave my white hanky of surrender, and submit to seek your face for guidance and direction. Amen.

PSALM 27:8

Stubbornness for Obedience

The struggle of not being stubborn, rebellious, unfaithful, and refusing to give your heart to God is a daily reminder there's a war waging between flesh and Spirit. God calls you out of the wilderness of pain for an opportunity to recover, while the flesh demands you remain stubborn and obstinate. You've been stuck in the depths of the most self-destructive terminal illness in the universe—the disease of *I,* with the enemy's nickname: *me.*

Oh, how you love to think it's all about you, sitting on the throne in the kingdom of me. The claws of it all about you have secured a death grip around your heart. Your feet are quick to rush into chaos and gossip; you stir the pot to get your way.

The spiritual warfare is extreme and intense because all of creation will bow and kneel to the name above all names—Jesus. The enemy wants to keep you off your knees. God's living word is your hope, and his lamp will light your way. Dare follow his light, and make it all about him.

Lord, I pray to leave my pathetic world of self. I am weary of all the consequences. I pray for courage to receive the new name you have for me. Amen.

PSALM 78:8; PROVERBS 6

The Big Picture

Powerless, you were weary and heavy-burdened, helpless, lacking purpose, with no hope for the future. The tumbleweed takes root and grows in the driest of conditions on the prairie. It appears dead, yet is alive. When a strong wind rips the tumbleweed from its foundation, it's sent on a majestic dance along the ground. It doesn't know its destination, yet is joyful with its new freedom. Its journey of tumbling freedom ends abruptly, stopped by a barbed wire fence. The tumbleweed sheds a tear thinking its life had no purpose.

A gentle whisper came with the wind, "My dear tumbleweed, your roots prevented erosion, and provided shade and safety for my small crawling creatures. With every tumble your seeds fell along the path traveled. Some will take root." The tumbleweed knew it had purpose.

You might not know your purpose or see the big picture while it's happening. Hold onto hope knowing there's a greater purpose for you than you can see at this time. Just don't quit.

Lord, I pray through patience and the comfort of the Scriptures, that I might have hope. I'm grateful that even when I tumble about, there's a purpose I can't see at the time. Amen.

ISAIAH 54:10; ROMANS 15:4

The Kingdom Is within You

Despite your past, the kingdom of God is within you. The Father gives you everything you need to be transformed by the renewing of your mind. You need to learn how to operate what God's entrusting you with, as a child climbing onto his first bicycle with training wheels. Begin to make good decisions during your pursuit of righteousness, peace, and joy. This is an imperfect journey and must be experienced as on-the-job training. You must trust the teacher, to be taught what you need to know.

Jesus revealed, by his actions at the cross, there's no greater love than to lay down your life for a friend. He encourages you to get out of yourself, not to be misled by the enemy's lie that you don't have time, and actually do something that's good.

Check yourself; is your recovery getting as much effort and time as your addiction once did? It's a lie from the pit of hell that you're unworthy and have nothing to offer. God honors you when serving him, and reaching out to those still lost in addiction.

Lord, I pray to be strengthened and not give up when discouraged or tired. I pray to do good things for you. Amen.

LUKE 17:21; ROMANS 12:2; JOHN 12:26, 15:13

Hiding Place

A few of the kids in the old neighborhood loved to explore the woods near one home. They looked for a place to build a fort and went to great extremes to keep it a secret—a hiding place to run to when they needed to get away. Kids would run to the hiding place where the wind's flow through the trees caused the leaves to play a peaceful symphony. Something deep inside told them if they just got to the secret place, all would be okay.

The enemy's secret place looks so good, yet after entering, the door of the concentration camp slams shut. The enemy is out to enslave you, while Jesus came to enhance your freedom. God encourages you to no longer live on the surface and embrace your day of grace and mercy.

With child-like faith, you soon discover the new secret place. God's Spirit within you becomes your new fort to run to. Recovery and healing are for you. When you're weary, don't give up! Run to your new fort!

Lord, I'm grateful you're delivering me one step at a time. I pray you bring to completion the good work you started in me. Amen.

MATTHEW 8:13; GALATIANS 6:9; JAMES 1:4

New Life in Christ

During moments of painful growth, where does strength to endure come from? The task might get done under your own power, but there's a sense of emptiness. In the flesh, it's uncomfortable when God takes you to the next level. It's essential to know where you've been and to see where you're going. You're in training with no graduation date. It takes commitment to stop using, endurance to go through hardship, effort to do what's needed, and persistence to recover, so your tests become your testimony.

The power of God saved and called you for his purpose, by the grace given you before the beginning of time. The enemy speaks, "I can't do it," through your lips, the counterfeit to truth. You can't survive in the enemy camp any longer and need to begin the pilgrimage to recovery.

Believe your new life in Christ is possible. Allow God to stir up the gifts already in you because if you're not stirred up or stretched, you'll never get to know your king.

Lord, I pray to hang in there when growth seems so painful. I'm grateful you saved me and stir up the gifts given me, even though I throw a fit at times. Amen.

2 TIMOTHY 1:9, 2:3; PHILIPPIANS 4:13

Keeper of His Promise

You've been wary of hearing anyone's promise; in fact, you've made many promises which were never kept. In recovery, you're brought face-to-face with the truth of God. Whatever he's promised, it's done, completed, and will come to pass. When someone disagreed, or challenged you on what was said, or even had a different opinion, you tapped out. Your action and behavior declare you know everything, and no one can tell you anything. Correction is not rejection—God knows more than you, and he sends people to correct you.

Every one of the Lord's promises to the house of Israel have been, or are being, fulfilled. He's made all his promises available to those who call upon his name. The enemy promises chaos and confusion. Whose promises have you been hanging onto?

You're an expert at being a strong starter out of the gate, but you lack fortitude to stick it out. Endure hardship and walk out your recovery to allow God's promises to become your own. So when you keep a promise you made, people won't be surprised.

Lord, I pray I will receive your promises as my own. I pray to honor and praise your great and awesome name, and be blessed with a good name, given and known only by you. Amen.

JOSHUA 21:45; 2 TIMOTHY 2:3; PSALM 99:3

Planned Recovery

It's a bit of a stretch when you enter recovery and hear someone tell you about the peace that surpasses all understanding. You've been trying for years to seek peace, and have always gotten chaos and confusion instead. In recovery, you're learning to be yourself, instead of being whoever people wanted you to be. Only in the glorious moment of ripping off the mask of your false self do you discover you truly cannot do this on your own.

God becomes very real when you truly know he's the one who saved you from yourself, because he loves you so. God takes your brokenness and begins reconstructing your life's puzzle pieces into the masterpiece he designed. He equips and strengthens you to do the good things he planned for you long ago.

God rubs out your guilt, washes away shame, and takes your sin as far as the east is from the west. God poured his special favor on you to walk out the recovery he planned for you long ago, one day at a time.

Lord, I pray I will continue, by grace, to experience your peace. I pray to walk out the recovery you planned for me long ago and not give up. Amen.

PHILIPPIANS 4:7; EPHESIANS 2:10; 1 CORINTHIANS 15:10

Expect His Promises

Your heart will be where your treasure is. This is a challenge because you were caught up selling yourself for much less than what God had for you. Jesus desires a personal relationship with you, at the moment of being unworthy of any good thing. God's asking if he can replace what you currently value with his Son. In recovery, God invites you to put an expectation on his seeds planted within you, rather than get twisted with what's worthless.

God's grace enables you to stay in step with him. You don't have to hurry; just remain in the lane God's placed you in. The land of the living is a good place to be, so you'll receive the harvest promised. What's most important to you—you and your circumstance, or God and his kingdom business?

When focused on self, you'll continue to get what you always got. It's critical to become willing to embrace the greatest treasure in the universe: God the Father, Son, and Holy Spirit.

Lord, I pray to not let my poor attitude and bad choices steal from me any longer. I pray to choose you, over myself, and expect your promises. Amen.

MATTHEW 6:19-21

His Work in You

Trust is a huge issue for everyone on this planet, especially those in recovery. God's Word is the only thing you can really trust. Trust in it, rely on it, and count on it to show you how to step into what he has for you to do.

God doesn't need your help, and whenever you hurry things up to do it your way, frustration opens the door to anger and a critical spirit. God can speed up time to expedite your circumstances and work out every detail into something good, with a lot fewer consequences.

When your attitude is right, God can pull you out of anything; yet, he allows you to experience what you go through to relate to what others go through. The tests and trials you face are to be considered pure joy. Each test and trial you allow God to take care of become tools to develop your weapons, so tests, trials, and temptations won't take you out. The Father will do what's best for you, to train you to pass each test and send a message of hope to others.

Lord, I pray to trust you more with my recovery. I love how you make my mess a message of hope. Amen.

ROMANS 8:28; JAMES 1:2

The Lord Will Rescue You

Each day brings you something that's needed for that day. When heaviness invades your day, things seem hard and you can't wait until the day is over. The enemy has twisted you to settle for another ordinary day in the life of shame and pain. You need to be on guard and not let your attitude keep you stuck. God's purpose for you is that you succeed in your recovery. Anything less is not from the Father.

Sorrow and sadness are your enemies. God desires to replace your ordinary with his extraordinary, and only he provides the light to rescue you from the wilderness of ordinary. Every attack against the God in you, appropriately handled, is another weapon to use on the black-op mission needed to keep your freedom intact.

The shepherd boy, David, was not afraid to face Goliath, and he quickly ran to meet him. The Lord who pulled you out of the pit will rescue you from addiction. How long has the enemy scornfully screamed at you with sarcasm, or insulted and ridiculed you? Trust God to cut off the heads of your giants.

Lord, I pray to be in the present moment, to see you more clearly. I pray to know my battles are your battles. Amen.

ROMANS 8:31; 1 SAMUEL 17:37-48

Grow in God's Love

Jesus declares his Father's law can be summed up in one command, "Love your neighbor as yourself." This is a trip for all in recovery because how can you be passionately tender with yourself, or someone else, when believing you're unloved and unlovable?

The remnants of the chains of slavery around your wrists and ankles linger for a bit. Believing the enemy's lie that you're unworthy of any good thing, much less love, you have nothing to give until receiving the unconditional love of the Father. This is essential to get, because God wants to love others through you.

About the only love affair you've got going is that you love to talk, reason, control, and figure out everything. It's your season to exchange that love for the love of God, love of self, and love of neighbor. To love God enough to serve him is to honor him. As you submit to receiving God's unconditional love, you're fertile ground for his love to grow in. It's your turn to experience total freedom as you leap into Jesus' arms to be loved, and the Holy Spirit fills your heart with love.

I pray I will drop the remnants of my loveless chains at Jesus' cross. I desire the freedom to love myself, and others. Amen.

LEVITICUS 19:18; GALATIANS 5:13; ROMANS 5:5

You Can Be Content

Just out of treatment you can be feeling so good; it's all praise and alleluia. You're redeemed, born again, renewed, and transformed, so you go skipping off... without accountability, support, or encouragement. Left to your own thinking, you're going down! Yes, God's got you, but you're a new babe in diapers going out to play linebacker in the NFL.

The old chaotic exterior will again invade your interior and demand participation. When content with where God's got you, the mask of your false self falls off with no resistance. It's okay to declare you're not going to hurt like this anymore. Don't be a pretender; you are worthy to be a contender.

You can be happy. Keep on praying, and in the bad times as well as the good times be thankful this is God's will for you. Be content where he has strategically placed you. Learn his truth and apply it in practical ways to your life.

Lord, I pray to keep moving forward, even if just six inches today. I'm thankful your will for me is to recover. Amen.

1 TIMOTHY 6:6; 1 THESSALONIANS 5:16-18

Ordinary Offering

Your spiritual worship is to offer your everyday ordinary life to God. This very act is pleasing to God and acknowledges his presence in your life. God left the most holy place to live in us. The world saw his ministry as a failure, his life ineffective: isn't this the life story of most of us coming into recovery?

Jesus offered himself for you in an amazing act of compassion. It's so powerful, you can't deny it. He desires intimacy with you, and he meets you exactly where you are with no limitations. When you admit you're poor, and crucify your pride at the cross, your healing begins. You've been saved from your past life of bad choices to choose life.

Deny yourself and take up your cross daily. Follow the one who climbed the cross for you. You've tried everything else and have nothing to lose. It's your season to recover.

Lord, I pray I will honor your sacrifice for me: dying so I might live. I pray to receive your love, so I can begin to love myself. Amen.

ROMANS 12:1; LUKE 9:23

Submit to God's Authority

You're a Jesus follower only as long as you stand, with gratitude, in the shadow of his cross. It's in this sacred place you can endure whatever comes. The enemy undermines the greatest act of love ever displayed by suggesting what God did as not being enough. God's truth declares this to be a lie from the pit of hell. It's God's Spirit that connects with your spirit to affirm you are now his child.

The flesh rears its ugly head, demanding attention, and attempts to resurrect itself daily in your thoughts, words, and actions. It wants to be in control, make decisions, and it absolutely hates to submit to God's spiritual principles. Fellowship with others who have been through what you've experienced is critical. They'll hold you accountable, encourage you when you're weary, and pray for you.

Together we are Christ's body, and each of us is an important part. Jesus purchased you with his own blood, so you can leave your kingdom of one to join God's kingdom.

Lord, I'm grateful that am no longer alone. I pray for grace to embrace those who guard, feed, and shepherd me. Amen.

ROMANS 8:16; ACTS 2:44, 20:28; 1 CORINTHIANS 12:27

Pointing Fingers

Most people struggle with the religious picture of God being angry at what they've done, judging them as unworthy, and punishing them by allowing bad things to happen. Heaven isn't an option because hell is the only place they deserve.

Truth mixed with lies keeps you confused and comfortable in chaos. The truth is that God so loved you so much he sent his only Son to die in your place. God's not the one pointing fingers of accusation at you, you are. He's got your eternal retirement package prepared—waiting for your signature.

God can pull you out of the worst situation when your attitude is right. This is where the rubber meets the road; it's your choice to accept God's unconditional love, experience the significance of Jesus' sacrifice, and claim it as your own. When you begin to live by his truth, you leave the darkness and enter his light, no longer fearful of exposure.

Lord, I pray I will keep admitting I don't have a clue. I pray to receive what you did, and claim it as my own. Amen.

JOHN 3:16, 19-21

What's Your Faith Tied To?

As you place your big toe into the ocean of God's great glory, you realize you haven't seen anything yet. God is able to do far more than you could ever imagine in your wildest dreams. His Spirit works in you tenderly and gently. When your day seems overwhelming and the enemy starts in with the lies, stand fast and speak to those lies, "God says I'm the beloved of his Son, and the best is yet to come!"

God's Spirit invites you to be made right with God. His gift, freely given, has nothing to do with what you've done. You've been searching for love all your life, and now the God of all creation tells you, "My beloved, here I am!"

Whatever you've done, you are not disqualified. Faith— believing in the unseen—is a stretch. But when you place your faith in Jesus, you tie your faith to his cross. Have faith that it's your turn to recover.

Lord, I'm so grateful you loved this black sheep into recovery. Thanks for the child-like faith that recovery is for me. Amen.

EPHESIANS 3:20; GALATIANS 5:5-7; ROMANS 3:22

Continued Survival

It's an absolute stretch to consider all problems and trials a time to rejoice. Especially in the moment. But they help you learn to endure, so you grow into the place where God desires you to be. Each time you're attacked, remember you survived the last one to the best of your ability. However this looks for you, be grateful you're still standing.

God is doing what's best for you, training you to share in his holiness, and harvest his peace. When trials seem overwhelming, with pop-ups and red flags every minute, don't allow circumstances to dictate your day. In the past, shame, guilt, impatience, anger, stress, and anxiety drove you into confusion and decisions which brought many consequences.

The point of any trial is to get through it so you become more mature. This is a work in progress. Spiritual warfare is about surviving until you place your head on the pillow to rest at the end of the day with gratitude and thanksgiving.

Lord, I pray you will help me to persevere through any trial which comes this day. I pray to not be so hard on myself when falling short. Amen.

ROMANS 5:3-4; HEBREWS 12:10-11; JAMES 1:4

This Day Is God's Gift

If lazy in recovery, you'll get put back to work in a relapse. Do you turn off the TV and get off the couch to go to a meeting which might save your life? This is not about last month, last week, or even yesterday: it's about this day being a gift from God.

God gives you an opportunity, today, to show your love and respect by allowing him to love another through you. It's a struggle to love others because you struggle to love yourself. It's easier to be critical, judgmental, and disrespectful because that's how you've treated yourself. Allow God's volcanic eruption of love to overflow from you onto others.

The Father desires to replace your stony, stubborn heart with a tender, responsive one. The peace of God will replace all your worries and anxiety. Just get to the next place you need to be!

Lord, I pray to be less critical and judgmental of myself. I pray for the courage to love others in the process of learning to love myself. Amen.

EZEKIEL 36:26; PHILIPPIANS 4:7

Faith and Actions

Ruffians who admit to being poor in spirit position themselves to receive righteousness from God. The story of Joshua and his armor bearer taking action, by faith, against an entire Philistine army is a majestic example of elevated confidence in believing nothing can hinder the Lord. God can win a battle whether he has many warriors or only a few.

God was not moved by Joshua's need, he moved because of Joshua's faith and actions. Your faith is critical; it will birth the same confidence and boldness Joshua showed by example. Faith in Christ allows you to go boldly into God's presence for whatever you need today.

Lay your recovery at God's throne and your faith will rise above the fear that another relapse will eventually take you out. Jesus asked his disciples why they were afraid. Did they still lack faith? Operate in faith that God's got your recovery, and move forward on your pilgrimage to freedom from addiction.

Lord, I praise you for the miracle that fear doesn't paralyze me like it did. I pray my actions make my faith complete. Amen.

1 SAMUEL 14:6; EPHESIANS 3:12; MARK 4:40; JAMES 2:22

Special Favor

A beloved hymn sings of nothing less than righteousness: a reminder you've lost nothing less than everything. God doesn't lie, change his mind, or fail to act. Whatever he promises, he will follow through to completion. If he hadn't allowed you to come to the end of yourself, you'd still be doing things your way. Be grateful for where God has led you.

Admitting you're poor in spirit strategically positions you to accept the righteousness available because of what Christ, the Messiah, did for you. You've witnessed God's glory in a personal way. Adrift and tossed by giant waves, clinging to a piece of what was once your ship of life, and a second away from giving up and letting go, God saved you.

You did not get what you deserved. Instead, he used that storm and shipwreck to reveal his purpose and plan for your life. God saved you by his special favor: his gift to you. Do you dare gift yourself back to him?

Lord, I'm very grateful you answered my cry and saved me. I pray for courage to gift myself back to you, to fulfill your purpose for me. Amen.

NUMBERS 23:19; EPHESIANS 2:8

Faith Makes Things Happen

Faith generates miracles, while doubt encourages tragedy. The only difference between today and yesterday is your faith, which gives birth to hope. As your faith begins to burst forth from God's seed sown deep within you, you dare to embrace his authority. When God speaks, he acts! Whatever he promises, he does!

It's seems a bit strange that we can expect so much from others, and yet, expect so much less from the creator of the universe. God doesn't have a problem with you living with expectancy of what he is going to do for you. God desires for you to receive healing.

Ask God to remove the blockage and limitations that keep you captive. He wipes away the deep hurts of betrayal, regret, neglect, and abuse with the blood-soaked rag of his Son. Expect him to do it, and it shall be done! In fact, it's already happened; God's just waiting for you to get there.

Lord, I pray you fertilize and water my tiny mustard seed of faith. I'm thankful my expectations of you never let me down, because you always exceed what I hope and pray for. Amen.

MATTHEW 21:22; I CORINTHIANS 4:20

Excuses Clog God's Aqueduct

In recovery, your flesh continues to rebel against the truth that God's ways and thoughts are higher than yours. Your reasons and excuses for thinking you have all the answers clog the aqueduct to the throne room of the most high God. Your connection gets so filled with gunk, God's purpose and plan for bestowing blessings on you are hindered.

So busy crawling on the floor, settling for the crumbs of life, you've unknowingly restricted the flow of God's living water to produce the fruit he desires to bring forth in you. You need someone to remind you God's ways and thoughts are life-sustaining.

God's bigger than what you've done, greater than your past and present, and he has secured your future. In the flesh, you've got another relapse. Call on the Lord while he is near. This is your season for recovery. Stay another day!

Lord, forgive me for the many times I seek myself before seeking you. I pray your clog cleaner keeps a clear connection to you. Amen.

ISAIAH 55:6-9

Don't Take Your Pardon Lightly

The judge and jury pronounced the prisoner guilty for the crime, and sentenced him to death. He had the famous last meal, walked the green mile, and was strapped into the electric chair. As the executioner grabbed the lever, the red phone rang to inform the warden that the condemned prisoner had been pardoned.

You're the condemned prisoner, Jesus is the advocate, and the judge is God. No one else matters. God is a just God, and he upholds his laws, principles, and promises. The devil comes before God to accuse you of your crimes, and you're guilty without a doubt. A merciful God calls across heaven to see if anyone will represent you.

Jesus steps forward: "I will represent him, Father. I took his guilt and shame to my cross. In fact, I died to set this man free and my blood washed all his sins away." God smiles and pronounces you *not guilty* because of his Son's sacrifice.

Lord, thanks for being my advocate and saving me from the executioner by taking my place. I pray I will get close enough to you to hear your whisper. Amen.

Love Always Wins

Many experience religion as a list of dos and don'ts, and they work hard hoping to qualify to be worthy of heaven. In recovery, you're learning the worst day of your life with Jesus is better than the best day without him. Truth spoken in judgment is totally ineffective; however, truth spoken in love is a game-changer. Love fills the God-space you've tried to fill with other stuff for years.

It's critical that your eyes see love in action and your ears hear words of love spoken. The wonderful, astonishing, amazing, and never-ceasing love of the Father is based on nothing you do. If it were, you would spend your recovery striving to qualify, and beating yourself up when you fell short.

You're not worthy; it's God who declares you're worthy, and he urges you to live a life worthy of the calling you've received. You can see his path to your destination, and hear his whisper that you're doing okay. Relax a bit, and receive the love freely given.

Lord, I pray for ears to hear your love language. I'm so grateful I don't have to earn your love—it would be a disaster. Amen.

MATTHEW 13:16; EPHESIANS 4:1

Make God's Purpose Your Purpose

Everything, absolutely everything, was started by God and finds its purpose in him. Begin to trust you were born by his purpose, for his purpose. God's asking you to walk into what he already has for you. As it becomes a bit less of you, and more of him, you suddenly realize it's already happening without much effort on your part. To know God is with you even during your most difficult days allows his grace to cover every situation.

As you leave the busyness of anxious thoughts, step beyond self-pity, and distance yourself from the heaviness of today, the should-, could-, and would-haves lessen in intensity. With childlike faith, you know Jesus' blood is the liquid grace seeping in to touch, encourage, renew, restore, and heal you.

Lighten up and give yourself a break; this is a *journey* to his perfection. Just don't give up, give in, or go back to what's familiar. That's not God's purpose for you.

Lord, I pray, with all that's in me, to walk into your purpose for me. I pray you will guard and keep me in your constant peace. Amen.

COLOSSIANS 1:16; ISAIAH 26:3

Wisdom to Trust

The key component of your faith-based recovery is accountability. It's especially needed when you become complacent with your recovery. God sends people to help you stay on track. The great danger of stumbling into relapse is when the old thinking creeps back in: *I've got this.*

It's critical to rely on others for guidance, counsel, and correction without being offended. They are there to assist you in staying out of slavery! Even though your flesh will rebel against sharing your dark secrets, your recovery and life depend on it. The easy path will always seem more inviting.

Now that God has made himself known to you, the enemy desperately wants to bring you back to your weak and miserable principles. Are you absolutely willing to do what you don't want to do, to do the things you need to?

Lord, I pray that insanity loses its appeal. I pray I continue walking in your freedom.

GALATIANS 4:3, 9, 5:1

Joy and Peace

This day is an absolute miracle. Seriously, you shouldn't even be here. Abba Father's warm, tender, and loving heart begins to melt away the many lies of the enemy you came into agreement with, and you can now experience peace and rest. Praise God for his freely given gift, and tell others of the marvelous works he's begun in your new life.

Hope was given to give away. By the grace of God, you know the numerous puzzle pieces of your life are being masterfully pieced together to make you whole. As Jesus' blood begins flowing through your veins and arteries, your words and actions reveal God to others. Those still suffering need to see the hope of God through you, and have it overflow into their lives.

The battle is on: humble and selfless gratitude versus pride and selfish indifference. You're a gladiator for God in the arena: fight well!

Lord, I trust your peace today. I pray for the full benefit of the Holy Spirit's sweet, gentle breath of life to allow you to have your way. Amen.

PSALM 9:1; ROMANS 15:13

God Is Your Source

Many use recovery as a time to get back what was lost while in addiction. You've searched the ends of the earth for the peace you thought possible under your own strength. Seeking that which the world offered, and pursuing what you thought would bring fulfillment, was a fast lane to the dark emptiness your addiction took you to. Do you dare give up what you cannot keep, to receive something you cannot lose?

Don't become distracted or obsessed with money or material things. There is never a trailer full of possessions behind the hearse going to the cemetery. In recovery, you learn to be content with what you have because of God's great promise to never leave you. He's got your back!

The world cannot recognize the great truth that God gave you his Son, a priceless gift, so you can give your gift of obedience back to him. God frees you to receive his love which you can never lose.

Lord, I'm in awe of your gift of eternal life through Jesus while I was still in the enemy's camp. I pray for willingness to serve you. Amen.

HEBREWS 13:5; ROMANS 6:22-23

The Old Way Has to Go

Willingness to change does not come naturally. It hasn't been part of your lifestyle. Willpower didn't work when you wanted to give up your addiction. The release from it lies within confronting the why behind the what.

We all have character issues. Lacking character entirely will not sustain recovery. The defects of character must be addressed, and freedom comes only when asking God to take them. Since you've chosen this new life of recovery, allow the Spirit to work out the details in every area of your life.

All you've known are setbacks, relapse, and settling for so much less than what God's got for you. Blame and ignorance are no longer excuses, or reasons, to continue down the slippery slope. Remember, God saved you, and you don't need to go back. Your old way of life, rotten through-and-through, has to go. Let God complete the work he's already begun.

Lord, forgive me when the slippery slope seems so attractive. In the flesh, I lack character and pray for discernment that acknowledges what you say is best for me. Amen.

GALATIANS 5:25; PHILIPPIANS 1:6

Wait Patiently for God

Make every effort to discipline yourself in the area of self-control. The next thing to do in building the foundation of recovery, is to get to the next place you need to be. This is a huge challenge if we're lacking self-control and are extremely undisciplined. To stay the course, we learn to wait on him for direction, purpose, and answers to prayer. God sends confirmation to reveal we're on the same page.

Ask God to guide and teach you in truth. He alone is your hope. When you trust the Father knows what you're going through and hears your prayers, his Spirit comes against the desires of the flesh—instant gratification, instant demands, and instant answers to prayer. You learn to follow God's timing instead.

Pray to accept the things you cannot change. Know God's working on thousands of things for you at this moment, even if you only know of three.

Lord, I pray I will rest in you and wait patiently for you. I'm grateful for the orderliness you've brought into my life. Amen.

2 PETER 1:6; PSALMS 25:5; 37:7

The Way Ahead

God's doing a new thing for you, and he invites you not to dwell on the past. You've allowed shame from the pit of hell to dictate your present as well as the future. In fact, the enemy brings up your past, on occasion, just to see where you are spiritually. Don't look in the rear view mirror; keep focused on what's ahead. This isn't about where you've been; it's about where you're going.

Your heavenly Father has patiently waited to reveal himself to you, and release his unmerited favor and grace upon you. As you become more willing and aware of the vital importance to do it God's way, it's essential to remember how far he's already brought you. Change is critical for your next breath, next step, and for your actions to speak louder than words.

God makes a way and provides streams of living water to nourish you. When you remember the desert wasteland you used to live in, and guilt and shame twist you to think that's what you deserve, God reminds you he sent his Son to die for you, so you can live abundantly.

Lord, I pray to keep focused on the way ahead. I'm so grateful for your tender mercies and unrelenting grace. Amen.

ISAIAH 43:18-19; JOHN 10:10

Enjoying Creation

One of the many gifts of your new life in recovery is the blessing of thinking clearly. It's as if you walked out of the oppressive, lifeless fog, where clarity was non-existent, into God's new dimension: breathing fresh, sweet, clean air of the highest quality. Flowers are painted in the deepest hues alongside flowing water gurgling and rushing to its destination.

Think clearly and exercise self-control; you were lost, and are now found. You've arrived at the place God has already prepared for you—the very presence of the Father's creation. As you set your hope on Jesus, you begin to look forward to his special blessings.

You've been here before without noticing where you were. The author of confusion and chaos tricked you into believing you were unworthy of having a chat with Jesus while walking through his beautiful meadows and fields overflowing with abundance. Now, the blessing of a clear mind gives you the choice to trust his new dimension is the place for you. It's your turn to stick and stay. Confusion no longer has to be where you are.

Lord, I pray to walk in your fields of abundance, rather than the enemy's lifeless desert of nothingness. I pray to listen to your wisdom with clarity, instead of reacting to chaos with confusion. Amen.

1 PETER 1:13-14

God Delights in You

What a whirlwind of emotions you experience during trials of life's situations and circumstances. At peace on solid ground and, out of nowhere, a severe thunderstorm of life with huge hailstones hits hard. Your foundation is shaken by an earthquake, which causes a shifting of the rock. There you are, one foot on solid ground, and the other on the moving ground; you're doing the splits.

Only God can keep you when chaos hits; he will open your blind eyes, free you from captivity, and release you from the dungeon. No longer blind, you identify what's coming and going, joy and despair, peace and conflict, faith and doubt, conviction and captivity, trust and distrust, victory and victim, prosperity and poverty, promises and twisted lies, just to mention a few.

God is the potter, shaping you in his hand for the good he intends to do for you. God rescued you because he delights in you.

Lord, I pray to no longer follow my stubborn heart. I pray for the courage to wait, yield, and be still while you shape me. Amen.

ISAIAH 42:6-7; JEREMIAH 18:6, 10, 12; PSALM 18:19

No Such Thing

Locked and loaded into addiction, ignited by shame, depression, and condemnation, you were absolutely clueless of the spiritual war raging around you. Events in life were labeled accidents, fate, bad luck. Fear ran rampant, fables and superstitions stumbled continuously through the brain, craziness combined with imagination flourished, mythology was accepted as truth, and agnosticism and atheism seemed the way out.

The enemy was working non-stop in his attempts to keep you isolated and in bondage. Pride and ego demanded to do it their way.

Your struggle is not against flesh and blood, but against the spiritual forces of evil in the world. Get to know who's out to kill your purpose, steal your joy, and destroy your hopes and blessings. Then fight back with God's Word.

Lord, I need you. I am not strong enough to fight this fight on my own. I'm grateful you claimed me and your Spirit is a deposit guaranteeing my inheritance. Amen.

EPHESIANS 1:13-14, 6:12

Believe and Anything Is Possible

The words *unfathomable depths* describe Jesus' relentless pursuit to shower his tenderness and mercy on you. It's so deep it cannot be measured by any human nautical unit, and it is available for anyone who seeks and accepts him, desiring intimacy with him.

As you begin to journey the path of his tenderness, your most difficult challenge is to accept yourself for who you really are: a human being, poor in spirit, in dire need of a Savior. Jesus walks with you. He invites you to come as you are.

To be tender with yourself doesn't have a lot to do with you or your efforts. It's an acceptance issue based on trust. As you receive Jesus' tenderness by whatever faith you can muster, you respond to his love by trusting him enough to give him your shame, guilt, resentment, and shortcomings. Jesus' compassion knows no boundaries, his grace has no limits, his mercy surrounds you, and he gives himself to those who call out his name. Anything is possible if you believe.

Lord, I'm blown away by how much you desire a relationship with me. I pray to give myself to you, as you gave yourself to me. Amen.

LEVITICUS 26:12; MARK 9:23

The Word Was God

The Word of God is sharper than the sharpest knife, cutting deep into your innermost thoughts and desires. Truth exposes you for who you really are, and comes against the intellectual genius, or a grand philosophy for a "new age" way of life. Scripture is God-breathed, living, active, vibrant, and life-changing. The Word is revealed to you by the Spirit of God.

The Bible is not to be confused with any other book on the planet. It's the only book which softens hardened hearts and opens eyes that are blind. Study it to know who the Father says you are. God's Word thoroughly equips you for every good work, and to confront confusion, disarray, lack of concentration, and wavering faith.

You've followed yourself and know how that worked out. It would be of great benefit to follow the one who knows everything. Only God has the answers to every question you've ever asked. You can always go back to what you had!

Lord, I'm grateful your Word has revealed your great love for me. I pray that I don't become lukewarm when it comes to reading your Word. Amen.

JOHN 1:1; HEBREWS 4:12; 2 TIMOTHY 3:16-17

Nobody into Somebody

Think of what, and who, you were when God called you into recovery. When you thought you were somebody, your actions declared you were foolish by human standards. The only thing you had was an addiction. The reasons, excuses, and blame have to go as you confront your false self. What the devil used to demote you, God turns around and uses it to promote you.

You did not choose God; he chose you. You struggle with even getting chosen. *Who would even want me, after all I've done?* After living a life of agreeing with who the devil says you are, you need to get into God's Word to get in step with him. You can't force anything under your own strength; your recovery comes about through his Spirit.

God chose you to produce fruit by your actions. Rejoice! You're in a good place. You had to go through all you experienced to get to the point of trusting his way more than your own.

Lord, I'm grateful you chose me. I pray I will be willing for you to promote me one step at a time. Amen.

1 CORINTHIANS 1:26-27; JOHN 15:16; ZECHARIAH 4:6

God's Light Makes You Glow

Oh, how you tried to separate yourself from God's love: weary and heavy burdened with shame, guilt, and pain. In spite of all your efforts, God's given you this sacred trust—to proclaim, by your example, his powerful message of hope to others.

Rather than use yourself for your purpose, God equips you to use yourself for his purpose. He promises not to change his mind about you. Say no when the enemy invites you to dance with him in secret and shameful ways. Truth set forth plainly chases deception back to where it came from. God's truth makes you glow.

You no longer have to walk on eggshells, beat around the bush, or tell others what they want to hear. Your example of living a life of transparency becomes your testimony to everyone you meet. God changes people-pleasing into a desire to please him. Embrace being a bit tender with yourself.

Lord, I pray I will please you rather than people. I'm so grateful for your sacred trust to tell others about you. Amen.

1 CORINTHIANS 9:17; 2 CORINTHIANS 4:2,6

God's Great Love

God protected you because of his vast, immeasurable, unconditional love for you. Who else could ever be passionately tender with you, while you were locked in chains of slavery to your addiction? When looking in the enemy's mirror, all you could see was *Unlovable* tattooed on your forehead. But, God's living Word penetrated your prison of lifeless nothingness.

Take advantage of the blessed door of opportunity to recover, and step across the threshold. God gives you his Spirit to empower you. This absolutely cannot be figured out with intellect or reasoning. You cannot earn it. An ordinary day becomes an extraordinary day when God's tsunami of spontaneous love flows freely into, around, and through you.

As you accept God's love, accept yourself as you truly are. When you love another, God lives in you and his love within you grows even stronger.

Lord, thanks for making me worthy to receive your love. I pray I will get out of my comfort zone and share your love with others. Amen.

ROMANS 5:5; 1 JOHN 4:12

Not the Easy Way

You're in danger of stumbling into relapse when tempted to go it alone, making decisions without seeking counsel. You were so desperate to get into a safe place, yet after a few weeks, or months, the old thinking creeps back in and begins to take up the space in your head.

Accountability to others is the key to keep from turning back to those weak and miserable principles which defined your past. You need to tell on yourself. The easy path will always seem inviting because in the flesh you're controlled by your old nature.

It's your season to do what you don't want to do. God sent his Spirit into your heart. Embrace these special days, months, and years to walk as a child of the most high God—one baby step at a time.

Lord, I pray for courage to seek you first, and do it your way. I pray for grace to walk into being your heir. Amen.

GALATIANS 4:6-10

Celebrate Losing Everything

You've lost nothing less than everything, which is a great place to be. Make it a clean slate and give God the stuff you cling to from the past: fear, doubt, anxiety, depression, and resentment. God has literally saved you from yourself. All you need to do to receive it is declare, "Jesus is Lord," and believe the Father raised his Son from the dead.

God has a huge purpose and a plan for you; his gifts and his calling on your life are irrevocable, with an eternal warranty. Instead of people running from you, they will be attracted to the God in you. Your words will not be spoken from intellect, but the Spirit of your Father speaking through you.

God saved you by gifting you his special favor when you first believed. The only difference between yesterday and today is your faith, which gives birth to hope and generates miracles. The Father desires to heal and wipe away your deep hurts if you dare to lose everything.

Lord, I pray you will remove the limitations I've put on my faith. I pray for grace to celebrate losing everything. Amen.

ROMANS 10:9, 11:29; MATTHEW 10:20; EPHESIANS 2:8

Greater than Your Past

When you pray for God's thoughts to be your thoughts, it causes a huge collision between your flesh and the Spirit. God's ways are so much higher than yours. Resentment and unforgiveness issues restrict your connection and flow to him. You can be so busy crawling on the floor for crumbs, confused and distracted, that God's living water ends up in a holding tank waiting for you to tap into it.

God's bigger than what you've done, he's greater than your past, and he wants to bless you today. Your future is secure in his hands. You've got it in you to hold nothing in reserve and shut down everything else to hear his whisper and respond. It's your turn right now; later will be more difficult.

This is God's appointed time for you to take full advantage of your opportunity. God desires you to live in joy and peace, and rejoice when the mountains and hills burst into song. Don't give up!

Lord, I pray for a clear flow of blessing from you. I pray to leap when I hear your whisper. Amen.

ISAIAH 55:6, 9, 12

Spirit, Water, and Truth

The cross is foolish to those who are perishing. It rattled the world that idolizes the human brain and expects to have all the answers. What intelligent person could even comprehend that a victim of Roman punishment and Pharisee legalism put to death on the cross could save anyone. The so-called King of the Jews did the impossible!

The keepers of his law didn't know him, but God was pleased with the foolishness of what was preached to save those who believe. God's testimony is greater than man's because it's about his Son. Jesus came by water and blood. His Spirit testifies because the Spirit is truth.

Greeks, Jews, tax collectors, prostitutes, and countless others were transformed by the wisdom of the cross, and its power remains to this day. Your thinking sputtered at the cross and couldn't save you, but the blood of Jesus cleansed you from all sin. Your days of playing games are over. Let God's testimony become your own.

Lord, I love your foolishness so much more than my intellect. I'm so grateful, Father, you loved me enough to send your Son whose shed blood washed me clean. Amen.

1 CORINTHIANS 1:18-21; 1 JOHN 5:6-9

The Recovery Marathon

In recovery, you no longer need to run away when feeling unsafe and threatened. You could qualify for the Olympics with all the running you've done in the past. Now, by God's grace, you run the recovery marathon already marked out for you with perseverance. You run toward God's finish line rather than away from yourself or others.

What Jesus did for you can be likened to a soldier jumping on an enemy grenade to sacrifice himself and protect his buddies. He endured the cross, and took the hit, to save you.

Jesus promises those who listen to his voice and follow him receive eternal life. You are secure; no one can steal you out of God's hand. It gets messy when you're overreacting to emotional complications; you may begin to free-fall towards that bottomless pit. But Jesus' safety net catches you. Get back in the race, and finish strong!

Lord, help me confirm your invitation to me so I will never stumble or fall. I thank you for protecting me.

HEBREWS 12:1-2; JOHN 10:27-30; 2 PETER 1:10-11

The Challenge of Intimacy

As you trust God to give up your addiction, his presence flows into the new available space. Child-like faith, like a seed planted in rich soil, grows. The pilgrimage of intimacy with God is a challenge. The most private and personal relationship you've ever had, and did whatever necessary to protect, was your addiction. If you can relentlessly pursue that which got you into the mess, you've got it in you to crawl up into Jesus' lap to rest.

God got the attention of Saul when he was on his way to Damascus. He was on a search-and-destroy mission against Christians. God revealed there that his mercy can save the worst of the worst. He took someone who was killing his people, and chose him to spread the Good News.

There's no denying God's mercy, grace, and patience on this deal; and what he did for Paul, he desires to do for you. Allow him to shape you from your worst to his best.

Lord, I pray I will remember the day you knocked me out of the saddle to save me. I pray I will excel in the grace of giving back what you've given to me. Amen.

1 TIMOTHY 1:15; 2 CORINTHIANS 8:7

Gift-Wrapped Recovery

Absolutely everything started in God and finds its purpose in him. Your personal pilgrimage in recovery is to discover God created all things and holds it all together. Your purpose is simply that you were born for his purpose. God loaded your recovery package by fitting together your broken and dislocated pieces.

You just need to start walking into what God's already prepared for you. To know he's with you wherever you go, even during the most difficult days, allows you the grace needed to walk out of your anxious thoughts, step beyond your pity party, distance yourself from the day's troubles, and quit arguing with yourself.

God's liquid grace continually seeps in, touching one molecule at a time, to encourage, renew, restore, and heal you. Get out of God's way and receive it. Remember, this is a journey to his perfection by extremely imperfect people. It's your effort, but his outcome—and you're okay!

Lord, I pray to continue my pilgrimage to you, the source of my life. Thanks for my recovery package. I'm so grateful your blood cleanses me. Amen.

COLOSSIANS 1:16-22

Listen More Intently

Your addiction can be transferred to believing life is all about you: what you want, and when you want it. So preoccupied with self, you dominate conversations by rambling on and on about your troubles. An obvious sign is interrupting others before they finish speaking, and showing a lack of respect by not asking how they're doing. This behavior absolutely grinds to a halt any opportunity for you to hear God's soft, still voice, or allow God's tender love to flow through you to another.

You've been saved from yourself. Get off your throne, and fully embrace the truth that God watches, protects, guides, delivers, restores, and gives sufficient grace to take your next breath, listen more, and speak less. There's a need to share, but also meet people where they are.

Begin using your ears more than your lips, hearing tenderly rather than dominating conversation. God held his hands out to you while you were disobedient and lost in addiction. Will you do that for another?

Lord, I pray I'll become a better listener, and interrupt less. I pray for courage to not block what you desire to do through me. Amen.

JAMES 3:9-10; ROMANS 10:20-21

Weakness and Hardships

Check out the mirror to see its reflection. Are you an imposter, pretending to be what you aren't, or authentic enough to admit who you truly are? The spirit of fear comes hard against love, and when it comes knocking to disrupt your day of being real, let faith open the door. Examine yourself to see if your faith is real or something abstract. The only way to fail this test is to not know Jesus is in you right now. If you fail the test, do something about it! When Jesus' love is in you, fear has to leave.

Are you willing to exam and take ownership of what's going on? There's a different road to travel than the road to self-destruction, medicating the pain of your resentment and regrets. It's okay to be hopeful!

Can you admit when you're wrong, or weak, quickly? The disciple Paul delighted in his weakness, hardships, and difficulties. It's okay to be driven to your knees by troubles; it's a great place to be.

Lord, I pray to endure whatever comes, for your sake. I pray when battered and bruised, your grace is sufficient to strengthen me. Amen.

2 CORINTHIANS 12:9-10, 13:5

The Shepherd Leads

In blind faith, combined with as much trust as you can muster, you begin to know wherever the Shepherd is leading you is a good place to be. Jesus is the gate for the sheep; the sheep hear his voice and come to him. He leads you out from where you've been surviving, to a place where you'll thrive. Wherever you go, you'll find green pastures and sweet smelling daisies growing abundantly. When you don't recognize the shepherd's voice, *that's* the stranger to run away from. There will be thieves and robbers who sneak around the flock; watch for them!

The Shepherd leads you to inventory the past and review today's troubles. When disagreeable or unexpected situations come during the day, Jesus walks you through, and out of, it. Withdraw and get to a place where you lay in green pastures, amongst the daisies, to hear the Shepherd's voice.

He reminds you he freely sacrificed his life for you. He has the authority from his Father to lay his life down and take it up again. The Shepherd leads you out and goes on ahead of you into recovery; follow him! You're worth this opportunity.

Lord, I'm grateful you opened the gate and saved me. I pray for discernment to know your voice more intimately. Amen.

JOHN 10:7-18

The Father Hears Your Prayers

Your feeble mind wanders while in prayer to the heavenly Father, especially during moments of perceived great need, rising stress levels, and bursting anxiety. God stands beside the needy, to save their lives from those who condemn.

In the midst of uncertainty whether the Father's even listening, or some remote chance he might not have what you're pleading for, his Spirit comes quickly to penetrate the battle in your mind. God gives hope and reassurance that whatever you need, or ask for, is already in the palm of his hand.

Don't get twisted into thinking that God is selective in who he listens to. He's no respecter of persons, and he will do for you what he does for anyone else. In fact, his Spirit will call chaos, anxiety, and counterfeit lies into the light when you can't identify them. You don't have to beat yourself up. Just get back up, dust yourself off, and run to Jesus' lap.

Lord, thanks for setting a time to enter your rest today. I pray I will trust that you hear and respond to my prayers. Amen.

PSALMS 109:31,112:4; HEBREWS 4:7

Dependency on God

If you think you're standing firm, be careful that you don't fall.
You're best when you're humble because that's when you are
praying. It's essential to know that your best thinking got you into
some extremely ugly and dangerous places. When you thought
you'd just got it, you missed it again, for the thousandth time.

This is all about confidence with humility. God's got you, yet
he desires your participation to walk with him his way, not your
way. For this very reason, make every effort to add to your faith.
You might not have known God, or didn't even believe in him,
but in that darkest moment, you cried out to somebody. It was
that instant, or down the road a bit, you came to believe it was
God who saved you.

If God took you from the deepest despair, why not give him all
you've got? God was training you for your season—a time to
channel your dependency on what's good. Dependency on God
is critical to your recovery.

Lord, I pray I will stay low with gratitude and thanksgiving. I pray
for grace to walk your way, not mine. Amen.

1 Corinthians 10:12-14; 2 Peter 1:5-7

Using God's Tools

We're not to just *go* through life; we're to *grow* through life. If you've fallen, or you're at the end of your rope, that's okay. This is where life begins anew. Get back up, push recovery's restart button, and get back into the program. God's already working on your behalf, for your good.

Your perseverance and not giving up is the story God's writing for you, and it hasn't ended yet. Don't quit! Use the tools God gave you to recover: the Bible, devotionals, and the materials from good addiction-breaking programs. Check in with your accountability partner every day, and attend the meetings you need to attend.

Over the years, you may have thought that having a Bible wasn't cool. You may have even felt embarrassed about carrying one around. Having a crack pipe in your mouth, spending three days in a casino, going through another detox, or spending a week alone in a hotel drinking and puking—*that's* not cool. Study God's Word and concentrate on doing your best for him. This is work you won't be embarrassed or ashamed of.

Lord, I pray I will use the tools you gave me to recover. I pray to be productive and effective in my knowledge of you. Amen.

1 CORINTHIANS 10:10; ROMANS 12:12; 2 TIMOTHY 2:15; 1 PETER 5:8

Anguish or Rest?

Anxious, tense, distracted, running out of time, having trouble sleeping... these all fall under being tricked into recovering in your own power. The enemy's out to numb your mind and twist you to become irritated, judgmental, easily offended, and confused, so you will medicate again. It's critical to know the enemy can only be effective when you agree with his lies.

When your feet become heavy, your insides are drying up from the heat of anxiety, and depression is inviting you to participate, there's only one place to find relief and rest; his name is Jesus. He lets you rest in green pastures.

The promise of entering his rest still stands. Jesus invites you to come to him when you are weary. You have two choices: to be tired and anxious, or to rest and find peace! Fight to enter the place of rest that only Jesus can provide.

Lord, I pray for your courage to resist the enemy. I pray I will rest in your lap more often than I have been. Amen.

PSALMS 13:2, 23:2; 1 PETER 5:8; HEBREWS 4:1; MATTHEW 11:28

Who Threw You into Confusion?

It's not about *if* temptation comes, it's *when* it comes. In fact, the enemy gets a lot of blame for stuff when it's simply the decisions your flesh makes through you. You need to be reminded that your flesh is stubborn and hostile to God. It cannot grasp spiritual principles, demands physical proof, and absolutely rejects the truth of God's approval of you.

You were running a good race; who cut in on you and kept you from obeying the truth? The one who's throwing you into confusion will have to pay the penalty. With rigorous honesty, you identify who's causing all the confusion and chaos—and find it's you!

Your choices caused many consequences for you, and others were deeply affected and hurt by your past actions. You were addicted to confusion. You need to get to know yourself to identify who you're feeding—the flesh or the Spirit. Today, don't hurt yourself, or others, by a decision made out of emotion.

Lord, help me remember where I came from and how bad it was.
I pray for perseverance, as it adds to my faith. Amen.

Mark 14:38; Galatians 5:8-10; 2 Peter 1:6

Jesus Gave You His Glory

As you pray to the one who saved you, you're overwhelmed by the glory Jesus gave you: the same glory the Father gave his Son. It's only in the Spirit you can understand that his glory in you is like dynamite destroying the strongholds, iniquities, and generational curses that held you in bondage for so long.

Jesus prayed that the disciples be one, as the Father and Son are one. God desires a close and extremely intimate relationship with you, and for you to know there's nothing you can ever do for him to love you more or less. As you receive God's unconditional love, it begins to penetrate deeply within your inner core.

God wants to free you up to free others. It takes a freed man to free a man. God's grace makes you more productive and effective. When you're busy doing his work, he can even give you a full night's rest with only 4-5 hours of sleep. Amazingly, you'll smile at the most irritating people when God reveals they're the very person you need to be around.

Lord, your face I will seek. I pray your glory in me will show others your great love for them. Amen.

JOHN 17:22-23; PSALM 27:8

Default Button

A huge challenge in recovery is the willingness to ask God to re-program your inner software so you feel safe and unafraid. Fear visited you frequently in the past, and it still checks on you from time to time. In your darkest moments, the Holy Spirit whispers to not be afraid or discouraged. God will strengthen and help you.

Walking on eggshells, not wanting to fail, and wondering if recovery is for you, is all fear. When you're fearful, it's easy to hit the default button and go back to what's familiar. The Holy Spirit empowers you to stay in what's unfamiliar. You no longer need to react to the dark cloud that's threatening to descend upon you. Rather than a curse, it's a blessed opportunity to trust.

God's hand will guide you, and he will hold you fast through any situation, as your once unsteady legs become stronger. Be transformed by trouble, rather than defeated by it.

Lord, I'm grateful you use everything I've done for your good.
I pray your love continues to chase fear away. Amen.

Isaiah 41:10; Psalm 139:10

No More Shame

Disgrace, condemnation, humiliation, and scandal, are synonyms for the word *shame*. When coupled with guilt, shame is a deadly, toxic cancer that attacks you relentlessly before recovery, and can revisit you any time.

God told Adam to eat any fruit except from the tree of knowledge of good and evil. He created Eve too. They were both naked and neither knew any shame. The serpent asked Eve if God really said not to eat from that tree. After more deception, she ate the forbidden fruit, gave it to Adam, and he ate. Shame appeared for the first time on this earth. Suddenly, they felt the need to cover their nakedness. They heard God walking in the garden that evening, and they hid.

Shame makes you cover up and hide. You've worked so hard to cover-up your shame, pain, and guilt of the past. You hide from others, from yourself, and from God. You agreed with the lie that your addiction would provide relief, and hid your shame and deep pain. Jesus came to take your shame upon himself at the cross. There's no more shame and no more hiding; you're now a child of light.

Lord, I'm grateful you took my shame away. When the serpent asks if you really did that, I pray for courage to respond with a resounding, "Yes!" Amen.

GENESIS 2:15-25; 3:1-10

Walk with the Wise

There's danger when gratitude decreases and complacency increases. When you are no longer diligent, your willingness ends up in the dumpster. The bright and beautiful spring and summer colors that were there when you first entered recovery fade into fall colors, which are still pretty, but the leaves are now dead. In a flash, the winter gray settles in for a dark and lonely night. Your face even looks different.

Laziness sets in quickly. You no longer want to be real with those who can help you. It's easier to be with those who don't. You'll never rise above the company you keep, and no one can take you where they haven't been themselves.

The Lord disciplines and corrects those he loves. Stay in a successful relationship with a wise mentor and keep attending a church where God is alive. Do the next right thing for your recovery. Seek counsel only from those who are wise in the ways of the Lord.

Lord, I pray for the strength to keep my recovery in the spring and summer months. I pray for shepherds who can take me where I need to go because they're already there. Amen.

PROVERBS 13:12, 18:17; HEBREWS 12:6

Lift Your Eyes to the Hills

One the great smokescreens of deception the enemy uses to trap you is making you think you could have done more so your day would have been different. You're responsible for your effort, and God's in charge of the outcome. He already knows you fall short, and he invites you to trust that he will make up the difference. As trust in him grows, you discover many circumstances disappear, or turn around for the good, without you doing anything.

Your effort is put on hold when you allow the fear of failure, or your natural tendency to withdraw and isolate, to take over. The lies of the double-dealing, counterfeit, cheater assault your brain and confuse you. You think Captain Control from the pit can lead you into action.

By grace, shut down the endless chatter in your mind. In a reckless display of surrender, lift up your eyes to the hills, and find your helper. God is your strength; he enables you to get off the couch and move forward.

Lord, I'm grateful my help comes from you, the maker of heaven and earth. I pray I will stay less in the should-, could-, and would-haves, and leave the outcome to you. Amen.

PSALMS 27:14, 121:1-2

In the Firestorm

The Lord is your solid foundation. His shield surrounds you. God will not allow the intense attacks you experience without giving you sufficient grace to sustain you. It's critical to know you were accepted by God before turning to him, and he has already equipped you to get through any trial he entrusts to you.

God gently reminds you that you can be content in the worst situations because when you draw near to him, he comes close to you. If you whisper his name, he will answer.

When recovery seems difficult, don't give up, complain, or do it your way. Get to the restful place of being thankful for God's favor and blessings. Your half-empty cup will suddenly become a cup half-full. Regardless of your situation or circumstance, you're not in hell—that's where God brought you out of. By his grace you won't quit, fall, or give up when the firestorm of today threatens to burn everything.

Lord, I pray to run to your lap for rest more quickly than I have been. I pray for thankfulness when I start a pity party. Amen.

PSALM 3:3; JAMES 4:8; ISAIAH 43:2

The Back of the Bus

God's light breathes life into your hopes and dreams, as he gently brings them into reality. This is the fabric of faith, hope, and love: believe in the unseen, allow his eternal hope to spring forth, and receive the Father's greatest gift to you—his Son. The enemy's counterfeits are fear, hopelessness, anxiety, and the lie that you're unworthy to receive what Jesus did for you on the cross. God is bigger than fear. His grace unlocks your prison door, his love opens it, and his light kicks fear back to where it came from.

The challenge on your pilgrimage of recovery is to embrace God's plan for you to prosper, grow in faith, praise and worship him, and wait on him for the fulfillment of his promise to you.

To wait for his perfect timing, schedule, leading, direction, grace, mercy, and love is a stumbling block for many. Oh, how we hate to wait. Instant gratification screams for right now. We wonder why it's taking God so long to answer. Our timing didn't work out so well in the past; why not try his?

Lord, I pray I'll get out of the driver's seat, kick my ego and pride off the bus, and take my seat in the back. I'm grateful you're doing for me what I couldn't do for myself. Amen.

HEBREWS 11

Furnace of Suffering

God refines you in the furnace of suffering. You've endured severe suffering already, and you're still standing; however, much of the suffering was a result of the consequences of poor choices. In recovery, you've put your toes into God's living water. God can take everything you've done and use it for good. It's essential to no longer work out of your emotions nor allow your past hurts dictate your future.

Freedom comes when you embrace, own, and accept the past hurts, moments of torture, and times of betrayal. Each weakness and flaw is an opportunity for God to reveal his strength in your life. Your flesh will tell you to give up, but hope for something better tells you to keep moving forward.

All of your past experiences, pain, difficulty, disasters, and the devil's attacks are used to build character and kindle your excitement in knowing God is in control and your future is secure. Without this process, there's no progress.

Lord, I pray the struggle I'm in today is developing the strength I need to embrace tomorrow. I pray to patiently endure the furnace, especially when it gets turned way up. Amen.

ISAIAH 48:10; ROMANS 5:3-5, 8:28-31

Believe and Receive

When you lean on your creator for strength and courage, life radically changes. If you think you can do enough to qualify for what God has for you, you're greatly mistaken. Your track record isn't good when dealing with impossible situations. You were twisted to think you were in control and your way was the way to go.

Surrender and *submit* are words that assault the old belief system of doing things your way rather than God's. Have you suffered enough, endured sufficient hardship, experienced bitter pain, and been brought to your knees in total brokenness? Ask the Lord to restore you.

If you're sick and tired of being sick and tired, you're in a good place. Gather as much child-like faith as you can muster, and take another step on the path God set for you long ago. His way is absolutely better than yours.

Lord, I'm thankful you saved me. You take great delight in me and will quiet my busy mind with love, as you rejoice over me with singing. I pray for courage to believe and receive this. Amen.

Luke 18:26-27; Lamentations 5:21; Zephaniah 3:17

The Best They Could

In recovery, God reveals enemy strongholds and patterns of destruction in your life that Satan used to steal your blessings, kill your dreams, and destroy the legacy for your children. Similar to a medical history, write down the issues and patterns of your family's behavior. The enemy uses deceit and lies on you that worked on generations before you. You said you wouldn't be like your parents, or do to your kids what your parents did to you. Years later, you discover you have done exactly that.

By God's grace, you open the inner rooms locked tight for years. The enemy wants to continue operating as he has and protect the territory gained through the generations. As you let go, the opposition is so strong that the struggle seems hopeless. Don't give up, lose heart, or grow weary. In his timing you will be blessed.

Resist blaming, and forgive others, especially your parents. You don't *have* to; you *get* to. It's not a burden; it's a privilege. When you forgive, your heavenly Father forgives you, also.

Lord, I pray I will forgive myself so I can more freely receive your forgiveness and forgive others. I pray to be diligent in letting go of that which hinders me. I forgive my parents of what I held against them. Amen.

GALATIANS 6:9; MARK 11:25

State of Trouble

Distress was one of the many middle names the enemy gave you; defined as suffering, shame, and trouble leading to anxiety. God's your strength and fortress to run to in times of great distress. You're no longer alone; you have a place to go during intense spiritual warfare.

The Father's love declares your worthiness for refuge, and invites you to leave the chaos and rely on his strength to get to his fortress no matter what. This is where peace, which surpasses all understanding, comes as a cool, gentle mist sprinkling its fragrant vapor all around.

A longtime memory can begin playing like a home movie in your mind. As a child, you stuffed the hurt deep inside, and its entangled roots penetrated deeply because the enemy had convinced you that the abuse be kept a secret. God knows that what you kept hidden caused great distress in your life. As you begin living in Jesus, give it to the one whose peace guards your heart and mind, and rest.

Lord, I pray to run to your fortress during times of distress. Thanks for taking my distress and anxiety whenever I give it to you. I love the sweet fragrance of your peace. Amen.

PSALM 145:18; PHILIPPIANS 4:7; ISAIAH 26:3

Go All In

It's essential to become willing to follow every one of God's principles. This isn't natural and has never been your lifestyle. Are you truly willing to change how you deal with circumstances? Your willpower never worked to give up your addiction. Gratitude to God for saving you from the pit of misery will help change your old lifestyle—one of excessive misery. Only when you let go do you allow God to begin his good work in you.

To delay is extremely dangerous, as your lack of character will never sustain your new life in recovery. When you address the defects of your character and ask God to remove them, you're dealing with them instead of them dealing with you, as they have been for years.

There's only one thing to change: everything. Anything connected with that old way of life has to go. Shortcuts are nothing but setbacks. This is about going all in, not holding anything in reserve. No more chips in your back pocket in case things don't work out. Go all the way!

Lord, I pray for willingness to go all in. I pray to allow you to begin your good work in me and stay out of your way. Amen.

PSALM 119:33; PHILIPPIANS 1:6; EPHESIANS 4:22

Mutual Acceptance

When you become willing to surrender the yoke of shame and guilt to your Lord and Savior, you break the bondage which held you captive. Jesus came to free the captives, and only his power can smash the lies of the enemy. It's an orderly process; you surrender your yoke to him, and then take his yoke upon yourself. It's only in Christ you stand firm. God gave you another chance to recover. After surviving your past, why not embrace recovery?

It's a joyous occasion when your brain clears enough to know God's been with you every step of the way; yes, even standing beside you at the bar, on the corner, or in the casino. He never gave up on you. He allowed every heartbeat, kept his vision for you in the palm of his hand, and waited patiently for you to receive his irrevocable calling.

God made you and has wonderful things prepared for you to do. He accepts you as you are, and meets you where you are. He accepted you; try accepting him!

I pray for courage to stand for you. Thanks for protecting me for another chance to recover into who you say I am. Amen.

2 CORINTHIANS 1:21-22; EPHESIANS 2:10

Here I Am

Do you dare do as Moses did when the Lord called him from the burning bush: "Here I am!" God told him he was standing on holy ground. Your holy ground is a loving and safe environment, where you're accepted for who you truly are. Your history of praying to God is during times of trouble and strife while in the back of police cars, in detox, before the court hearing, in jail or prison, when sick in withdrawal, during the darkest of nights, and for one more chance.

God is available to you one thousand, four hundred, and forty minutes a day, every day, and he desires a personal relationship with you, with no restrictions. You no longer call on him just in emergencies; you can have a one-on-one with the one who knows everything anytime you dial.

Have you endured enough misery and heartache? Are you tired of getting what you always got? When God calls you by name, do you dare reply, "Here I am!" Be available to him. What have you got to lose?

Lord, I'm grateful your truth set me free. For from you and through you and for you are all things. To you be the glory forever. Amen.

EXODUS 3:4; JOHN 8:32; ROMANS 11:36

The Storm

God sends storms into your life. He opened the heavens and came down; dark storm clouds were beneath his feet. God plans to give you the opportunity to walk with him to the place he desires you to get to. The Lord hurled a powerful wind over the sea, causing a violent storm that threatened to break the ship apart. Storms give an opportunity for you to clean your plate, get priorities reset, and take what you can't let go of on your own.

Some storms are for his good reasons and work out for your good. Sometimes the devil sends the storm, attacking and repeatedly wounding you without cause. Some storms are self-inflicted; you've a sabotage expert for years. When you're in a storm that's seemingly relentless, many times it's the one going on in your mind.

Some storms aren't too bad until you react and think other people caused it. Storms form when you experience trials, tests, and sorrow. Get to know where the storm originates—is it from God, the devil, or you? Don't be surprised when wild and severe storms appear. How are you going to react?

Lord, I praise you for the storms you allow which give endurance a chance to grow. I pray for wisdom to know where each storm comes from. Amen.

2 SAMUEL 22:10; JONAH 1:4, 14; JOB 9:17

Refuge from the Storm

The most intense storms of life can last many months as you're sucked into the undercurrent of the whirlpool of self-pity while full of anger and blame. God sends storms to break us down. Confusion adds to the turbulence of a storm, yet God invites you to rest in his tower of refuge, and take shelter from the rain.

It's critical to know the difference between sprinkles, showers, and storms. The enemy exaggerates a light rain to appear as a violent storm. In a flash, you believe the lie that the storm's getting worse and you fear how terrible it will be. Overwhelmed, with a troubled heart, your anger at the storm turns into rage and you think your life will be blown away like a tent in a strong wind.

If your life is over, how are you still here? It's essential to know there's opportunity in the storm, and the best people to help you navigate a storm are those who have already survived other storms.

Lord, I pray I will listen to those who have survived the storms. I'm grateful you're in the eye of the storm and I don't have to run from it. Amen.

Isaiah 25:4, 38:12; Jeremiah 4:13

The Storm Forms

If you are easily offended, you'll always struggle. All authority is God-sent. Most storms come when we're offended by someone, especially those in authority over us. When acting as the hands and feet of Jesus, serving others, it's critical to know you cannot be effective and offended at the same time. Offense will hinder you from seeing the truth and loving another into recovery.

Whenever you stumble over Jesus, you're in the midst of a self-induced storm. Your entire perspective changes and knocks you off track of what God has for you, and where he desires to take you.

It's critical when feeling offended, and you will, to go directly to the source and talk to them about it. Don't run to others and spread the poison. If rehearsed and enabled, offense will become part of your response to just about everything, and the only person it truly hurts is you.

Lord, I'm grateful to know storms come when I'm feeling offended. I pray I will go to the source whenever offense comes, to talk about it and give it to you. Amen.

MATTHEW 11:6

Shaking the Tree

There are storms when you feel everyone has deserted you. God shakes your tree and those who fall to the ground are those you no longer need. There's nothing like adversity to reveal who your true friends are. When people abandon you during a storm, they're doing you a huge favor. Chances are they would have left later anyway. When the storm passes and you're still standing, those who laughed when you were in trouble, and mocked you when disaster overtook you, are gone. Don't be angry at them for leaving; be grateful they're gone.

People can be your shelter from the wind and a refuge from the storm, like streams of water in the desert and the shadow of a great rock in a parched land. God brings people into your life to help you distance yourself from the storm. You're at your best when all you have is God.

Storms also reveal you're an asset, not a liability. You're worthy to dig down deep and lay your recovery foundation on the Rock, which will not be shaken or moved. This is your guarantee you'll be okay during any storm.

Lord, if there's someone in my life I need to let go, help me. I pray to not run, but dance in the rain of the storm. Amen.

ISAIAH 32:2; MATTHEW 7:26-27; LUKE 6:48

Gift of Recovery

Humble yourself to praise God and thank him for saving you by the blood of the Lamb. This one act displays a radical transformation of selecting God's kingdom over yours, and submitting to an authority greater than yourself. Be in the presence of the Father when confronting your shortcomings and character defects. God knows your heart and has already started your housecleaning. As the Father massages your heart, you begin to care about people and what they're doing.

Naturally, your feeble brain can't comprehend the truth that Jesus made himself nothing, took the position of a slave, became human, died a criminal's death on the cross, and the Father raised him up, just to give you his eternal life insurance plan. Intellect and reasoning cannot fathom the depth of this revelation.

Jesus was humiliated, publicly shamed, tortured, and beaten so terribly he didn't resemble human form, to take your dirt and sins onto himself and pay your debt in full. He's your example of humility to follow. Jesus humbled himself to die for you, so you can dare humble yourself to embrace the gift of recovery he's given you.

Lord, I pray your death on the cross is sufficient for me this day. I pray for grace to receive your gift of yourself, and your gift of recovery. Amen.

PHILIPPIANS 2:3-8

Track of No Return

As you draw nearer to God, his presence and peace expose your character defects and shortcomings. God is light, and in him there's no darkness. He invites you out of the darkness of depression to share your secrets. The Spirit empowers you through the fear of letting go, and when confessing your sins, God is faithful to forgive you. He wipes your slate clean. The blood of his Son replaces the heavy yoke of shame on your shoulders with his robe of righteousness.

When you're in control, it's as if the flesh put handcuffs on God, making it impossible for him to do what he desires for you. Your addiction revealed, in a powerful way, your need for a Savior. You've never done anything halfway, and you were riding a bullet train headed for a final, huge wreck down the track of no return.

God's mercy and love gives you another opportunity to ask him to restore the joy of his salvation, and give you a willingness to do whatever it takes to walk with him into your healing.

Lord, I pray I will escape to you for rest and joy rather than medicating distress and sadness. I pray I will be thirsty for your living water. Amen.

1 JOHN 1:5-9; PSALM 51:10-12

Special Days

The enemy trained you to think your way was the best and only way. In recovery you discover your way was the way of stubbornness. You have a choice to no longer be like your ancestors: rebellious, unfaithful, and refusing to give their hearts to God. In truth, being unreasonable, bullheaded, and headstrong kept you in chaos and confusion. Pride and control are strongholds which you cannot come up against in your own strength.

You're now observing special days, months, seasons, and years on your pilgrimage to do it God's way, with renewed vigor and hope. The spiritual warfare between your way, and submitting to the Father's way is intense. It's your choice: keep believing the devil's lie that medicating your shame will dull the pain, or kneel to the name above all names—Jesus—who took your pain upon himself and gives you rest!

Only by God's grace are you open for correction and accountability as his lamp lights the way ahead of you. It's your special time to get this.

Lord, I pray you will save me from myself, to kneel before you. I pray your gift of this special time will be fruitful. Amen.

PSALM 78:8; PROVERBS 6:23

Plant through Tears; Harvest with Joy

Can you hear the music? Can you hear this song?
A different beat and sound, since you've been gone.
All around emptiness continues to persist,
Difficult to reason whether or not I exist.
Green grass turned to brown,
Birds chirping, yet heard no sound.
I cried, I died.

This ditty was written when life was hard, no hope existed, and addiction was claiming my birthright. You can relate to tears exploding from deep within and how the constant guilt and shame twisted you to think there was only one way to silence the incessant chatter of unworthiness.

When at rock bottom, with no hope or future, God locks you in a bear hug and won't let go. Tears held inside for years began as a trickle, and then flow freely. Jesus wipes your tears and reassures you that he's already taken care of everything.

The Lord waits patiently for you to need him. God's grace opens your ears to hear his laughter. Accept his invitation to dance as King David did, with all your energy. Haven't you experienced enough pain to finally let your tears flow? Jesus is patiently waiting.

Lord, thanks for restoring me, filling me with laughter, and singing for joy. I'm grateful for your promise that those who plant through tears will harvest with shouts of joy. Amen.

PSALM 126:2-6

Antagonistic

Why is it that when someone offers wisdom and advice, there's something in you that hates being told what to do. The flesh is opposed to the Spirit, and the desires of the Spirit are opposed to the flesh; they are antagonistic to each other. The battle between the flesh and the Spirit gets you, and everyone else on this planet, twisted in doing what's right, or doing what's wrong.

The apostle Paul struggled with his flesh all the time. He talks about the struggle of constantly doing what he doesn't really want to do. The flesh is antagonistic to the Spirit; it's hostile, opposed to God, overly sensitive, easily offended, and critical of others. It always takes you further than you want, and instead of proving others wrong, you prove them right.

Who will free you from the flesh? Thank God, the answer is in Christ Jesus your Lord. He calls you, equips you, and strengthens you to say no to the flesh, and embrace recovery.

Lord, I'm grateful your gifts and calling can't be withdrawn.
I pray to identify my flesh more quickly. Amen.

GALATIANS 5:17; ROMANS 7:15, 24-25,11:29

God Has the Answers

A father brought his son for healing. The disciples couldn't do it, yet the father didn't give up. In desperation, he asked Jesus to do something if he could. Jesus responded that anything was possible if a person believed. Isn't that what we say to God: "Help me if you can?" The challenge is to step out, to allow him to step in. Anything's possible, even for those guilt-ridden, lost sheep who have been beaten up by their past. Do you believe it?

As you seek first God's kingdom, he gives you everything you need to believe what's impossible for you is possible with him. The Father protected you to have this special time to recover. Believe that you can let go and let God. Admit you're powerless, your life is out of control, and you absolutely need God, because he's all you have.

Your questions now have answers: What about this? God's got it! What about that? He's already done it! What about them? He's working! What about yesterday? He's taken it! What about today? He's given you strength! What about tomorrow? It's already secure! Do you believe the answers?

Lord, thanks for answering all my questions. I'm overwhelmed to witness your blood-stained cross and empty grave to know you loved me that much, even during moments of my unbelief. Amen.

MARK 9:17-27; MATTHEW 6:33, 19:26

Do You Really Want Recovery?

You've got to get this—you're going to have to work one way or the other. Since you already know confusion, chaos, and pain are waiting for you out in the parking lot, why not at least experiment with a new way of doing things. A new day, a new you, doing the best you can to live a day of clarity, peace, and free of pain. You'll even welcome tests and trials during the day, knowing they were sent to test your faith and develop perseverance producing endurance.

The challenge is to allow the process to continue, and not to quit until you're on the other side of what's crowding into your life. Pride demands to make your decisions, yet you've experienced, many times, the consequences of complicating a mess without seeking advice or counsel. The world offers turmoil, insecurity, frustration, and distress. God promises perfect peace and confidence during any challenge you face.

Tests and temptations are opportunities for growth. Choose this day to work your recovery rather than working your relapse.

Lord, I pray to look at tests and temptations as growth opportunities. I pray for strength to go through challenges and grow through them. Amen.

JAMES 1:3-6; JOHN 16:33

Requirements of Addiction

Are you all in, or double-minded and unstable? In recovery, you're either moving forward, or you're going back to where you came from. If your drug dealer didn't answer, you called someone else. When a liquor store was out of your favorite Irish whiskey, you found it somewhere else. When told to leave a casino, you went to another. You didn't go halfway with your addiction, so go all in with your recovery.

As you mumble and grumble about the requirements for recovery, have you forgotten the extraordinary requirements of addiction? Working at recovery is critical; you don't know if you'll have another chance. Life on life's terms isn't easy, but you no longer need to run from it.

Being double-minded and unstable becomes a threat to your recovery when you entertain it too long. Get out of your busy mind, submit to God, and let him give you the strength you need to go all in.

Lord, thanks for coming near to me when I come near to you. I pray for grace to go all in with my recovery, because half measures avail nothing. Amen.

JAMES 1:7-8, 4:7-8; 1 PETER 1:7

Little Kid Issues

You're in trouble if you're making your own decisions. God gives you shepherds after his heart, who can guide you with knowledge and understanding. By grace, set aside your pride, say no to the flesh, and don't listen to the enemy's chatter about keeping everything inside. You don't want to be your own guide because you're in a place you've never been before. The Hebrew definition for *counsel* is *to plan*. You know how to plan to feed your addiction; you need help to learn how to plan your recovery.

You came into recovery with little kid issues. You need someone mature to teach you how to become an adult and encourage you along the way. This person can't be a co-signer, but will sharpen you. Your mentor needs to be able to speak directly to you, reminding you of what works in recovery.

Respect those who care enough to spend time with you; they're helping to save your life.

Lord, I pray a blessing over the shepherds you've sent me. I'm grateful I desire counsel before making a move, to avoid the consequences of wrong choices. Amen.

JEREMIAH 3:15; 1 CORINTHIANS 13:11

Time for a Fresh Spirit

It's crucial you trust that it's your time and season to receive a fresh spirit. The Holy Spirit gives you revelation, which reveals and searches out everything, showing you God's secrets. This provides the opportunity to check on yourself—is this from God, the flesh, or the enemy of your soul?

When united in God's Spirit, you'll experience peace in the midst of troubles. When feeling timid, you begin to rely on the power of the Holy Spirit because you are focused only on Jesus.

Spiritual truths can't be explained by knowledge; they sound foolish when you try to figure them out in your mind. Your prideful, egotistical self absolutely hates the idea of becoming a fool to become wise by God's standards. Your flesh demands to be in control, and the enemy comes to steal God's wisdom from you. This isn't about religion—it's all about relationship. You have an advocate who testifies to your clean slate. Quit looking in the rearview mirror, and enjoy a day in recovery.

Lord, I pray to choose the advocate over my prideful self. I'm so grateful when focused on you. Help me stay in your lap to rest a bit longer. Amen.

EPHESIANS 4:3; 1 CORINTHIANS 2:2-5, 10, 3:18-19; HEBREWS 10:17

Content Doing Good

Despite your past, and the many times you fall short, the kingdom of God is within you. It's one of righteousness, peace, and joy in the Holy Spirit. God gave you the full package; yet, like a child, you need to learn how to operate it, starting from square one with baby steps.

When you get out of yourself to serve Jesus by serving others, God's approves what you do on his behalf. Don't get tired, discouraged, or give up doing what's good. The Father promises you a harvest of blessings at the appropriate time.

The richness of your personal relationship with Jesus is in direct proportion to your obedience in serving him. This isn't about your actions earning you a closer connection with the Lord, or receiving recognition for all the things you've done. It's all about you choosing to do what's good and being content while you do it. Jesus, the greatest servant, invites you to follow him, because you need to be where he is.

Lord, I pray for courage to allow you to love through me. I'm amazed and thankful the Father honors anyone who serves him. Amen.

LUKE 17:20-21; ROMANS 14:17-18; GALATIANS 6:9; JOHN 12:26

God's Crusaders

As you begin to walk onto God's foundation of recovery, a light bulb moment of truth penetrates deeply to the inner core. The greatest act of service and love ever expressed in the universe was at Jesus' cross where he laid his life down. The Messiah did that before your birth, knowing all you were going to do, and go through, on this planet. God served you unconditionally by giving his Son for you. Do you dare lay your life down and serve him?

By the act of love from the Father and the Son, you're now worthy and have something to offer others. You're a crusader for his greater purpose. Check yourself to see if you're as serious about recovery as you were about your addiction.

There will be moments when you want to be noticed, recognized, congratulated, or thanked for a job well done. Oh, how the flesh loves to hear, "You're the greatest." That's okay, just know the great accountant in heaven is clapping and cheering whenever you love and serve one of his precious ruffians.

Lord, thanks for being my redeemer and choosing to love someone through me. I pray for strength to step outside of my comfort zone and be a crusader for you. Amen.

JOHN 15:13

Something More

Addiction was a miserable existence caused by what you were thinking, doing, and what you failed to do. It's a bleak portrait of a summer in darkness, when life seemed to be a waste and every breath a struggle. Guilt and shame, along with the spirit of fear, kept greasing the slippery slope for the rollercoaster of the flesh. Self-pity and condemnation, combined with issues of unforgiveness, deepened the depression. The many failed efforts to change your existence, in your own power, finally got you fed-up.

You needed something more, and obviously needed help to stop the power of sin within you sabotaging your best intentions. The enemy tricked you to become the enemy. The flesh is at war against the Spirit, and the powers of this dark, evil world are at war with you. It's critical to know your battle is not against people.

When you understand the truth of the power of Jesus' cross, help has just arrived to save you. Celebrate your broken road, as God used it to bring you to embrace him.

Lord, I'm grateful I don't need to sabotage your truth. Thanks, Jesus, for freeing me from a life dominated by addiction. I pray I will rest in you. Amen.

ROMANS 7:17, 25; EPHESIANS 6:12

Back on Your Feet

When you're focused on current circumstance, it's easy to become discouraged with anxious thoughts. Distracted, you stumble back on the fast track of figuring out the next move. When the road becomes bumpy and seemingly impossible, God encourages you to get back your feet and move forward. He's appointed you as his servant and witness. Your greatest witness to the glory and magnificence of God is by your example—the way you live. Your service is to love another in addiction, who only you can touch. Don't just believe in God, experience him!

Have you forgotten the moment your cry for help was answered? God took you out of where you were and got you into recovery. When you embrace the truth that you were rescued, and begin to walk as one rescued, God takes anxiety, and gives peace. By his grace, your spiritual eyes see exactly how far he's brought you, and your child-like faith gives you assurance about things you can't yet see physically.

You might not be where you want to be, but trust God to get you to the place he desires you to be, or you'll be shadowboxing again.

Lord, I pray I will remain desperate in recovery. Thanks for rescuing me. By your grace I will help rescue others. Amen.

ACTS 26:16; JOSHUA 1:5; HEBREWS 11:1

Nothing Less than Extraordinary

Worries and anxious thoughts set you up to have another ordinary day with feet encased in shoes of concrete. When feeling overburdened and overwhelmed, you impatiently wait for the day to be over. God's already prepared an extraordinary day of grace to strengthen you. You're looking at the old way at the same moment God is about to do something new; in fact, he has already begun. Rejoice, and enjoy the gift of the day he has for you.

Your flesh and emotions have been in control and made your decisions for years. In order to do something about it, you've got to stop doing what you've always done. You need to change only one thing—everything. In recovery, God's stretching you beyond any place you've ever been and it's uncomfortable. Be grateful he's creating rivers of new life in your dry wasteland.

When your flesh says, "I can't," God's Spirit in you whispers, "I can." When the enemy comes saying you're going to fail, the Spirit declares you can do all things through Christ who strengthens you. Enjoy your extraordinary day!

Lord, I pray while stuck in the valley of no-decision, to let my yes be simply yes to what you ask of me. I praise you for the grace to experience your extraordinary day when I want to settle for ordinary. Amen.

Isaiah 43:19; Matthew 5:37; Philippians 4:13

The Top of the List

When you're persuaded to put children before your recovery, that persuasion doesn't come from the one who calls you. If unable to be with your kids, give them the best gift you can—work on you. So many go back before they're ready, and they end up crashing and burning for the umpteenth time, leaving the children again in disarray, and with more consequences to deal with. Your past actions and behavior have hurt those closest to you.

When you pursue recovery with rigorous honesty, you become ready to let go of self-pity and being a victim. A victim mentality leaves victims in your wake. Your children have been affected by your addiction and don't need to be victims any longer.

God says you're not a victim anymore. Persevere in your recovery, so no one else needs to suffer your suffering. Don't drift along thinking you're okay when you're not. Recover for yourself, so you can be there for your children and not leave again.

Lord, I pray to keep recovery at the top of my list, so my family will be blessed. Thanks for the courage to ask others how my recovery looks to them, and the grace to listen to their suggestions. Amen.

GALATIANS 5:7-8; JAMES 1:4; 2 CORINTHIANS 13:5

Self-Examination Is Critical

You're an expert in pointing out other people's faults, and you can list their character defects instantly. This deflects what's really going on in *your* life; it's the counterfeit to self-examination. The Lord is near when you call out to him. It's his truth that frees you from blaming yourself, and makes you willing to face things you're ashamed of.

As you call upon the Lord, he walks with you through the guilt and shame, and helps you to keep moving forward. It doesn't matter where you've been; it matters where you're going.

Changing the way you live is a lifetime process. It's progress, not perfection—a marathon, not a sprint. It's extremely important to be thorough with self-examination, and talking in detail to your mentor to identify the source of what's been demanding medication. God will identify strongholds so you can do a military surgical strike to slice off the root with his sword of truth. Some strongholds in your life need the Heavenly-Mega-Bunker-Buster-Bomb, which God will release if asked. Freedom from the past comes only when you give it to God.

Lord, I'm so grateful your truth sets me free. I pray to be thorough when examining my motives. I need a lot of those bunker busters. Amen.

PSALM 145:18; JOHN 8:32, 36

Stay near the Truth

There's something coming every time you think you've got it all together. Your willingness for correction lessens, and if you're not open for advice or counsel, you start making your own decisions once again. Soon, excuses justify your behavior, and creep into the language you speak over yourself—stinking thinking!

It's critical for your recovery to position yourself to stay near the truth, which clearly identifies the lies of the enemy. God uses people to come around you and lift you out of the busyness of your mind. Share your thoughts with someone you trust to tell you the truth.

God's light illuminates the darkness of the abyss you came from; you don't have to go back to that murky, gloomy place of shadows. God's Spirit empowers you to fight through your stubborn flesh and the enemy's smokescreens to lie down in green pastures and be led beside quiet waters. Don't quit!

Lord, I'm grateful my intellect sputters at your cross. I praise you for washing, sanctifying, and justifying me in your name. Amen.

1 JOHN 1:9; PSALM 23:2-3; 1 CORINTHIANS 6:11

God Cheers Your Willingness

Peter responded to Jesus' call to get out of the boat, but seeing the high waves, he began to sink. Jesus rescued him and then asked Peter why he doubted. Peter was not judged or condemned, he wasn't asked to leave, and wasn't demoted to assistant disciple. The storm stopped, and when they landed on the shore, they went back to work healing the sick.

God delights in your efforts to go another step on the road of recovery. During a storm, are you willing to take a leap of faith out of your boat of limitations? Christ suffered for you, leaving an example that you should follow in his steps. He suffered everything that came his way for you to know how to endure your suffering.

His way is the best way through the storm you face today. Stand firm in Christ. He anointed you, put his Spirit in you, and stamped you with his personal, private mark of ownership. Jesus is still in the rescue business for those willing to leap out of their stormy situation.

Lord, thanks for your mark of security and guarantee of protection. I'm grateful my lifeguard walks on water. I praise you for getting excited over my feeble efforts. Amen.

MATTHEW 14:31; 1 PETER 2:21; 2 CORINTHIANS 1:21-22

Your Recovery Masterpiece

In recovery, you're being taught to exchange your former way of life for a new life: to be like God in true righteousness and holiness. Jesus did all the work when he became sin for you. You're now in right standing, and can be with God. This is about receiving what Jesus already did. Jesus begins to paint your recovery on canvas.

Experts have found great works of art sometimes conceal a painting underneath. Your new life is being painted over the old one. God does a quick work, yet it takes time to learn to walk in his promises and blessings. It's up to you to respond to God's invitation to place the dark and gloomy painting of your old life on the easel. His unconditional love will whitewash, in one masterful stroke, the old painting of shame and guilt.

The Father then gives you the paintbrush to record your daily walk of living a life worthy of the calling you've received. It's critical to allow God to paint through you, choose the colors, and have the chance to complete his masterpiece for your life.

Lord, I pray for obedience to allow you to paint my recovery because it will be a masterpiece—colorful and priceless. I pray for strength not to splash paint on the canvas just to hurry up and finish. I trust you to choose the colors. Amen.

EPHESIANS 4:2, 22-23; 2 CORINTHIANS 5:21

Visit the Manger

Christmas is a time of reflection and celebrating the birth of Christ—God's gift of love to you. His only begotten Son, Jesus, was born in the flesh and is Immanuel: God is with you. The gift you give him is an intense desire to pursue his presence. Who better qualifies to visit the manger than a ruffian, battered and bruised, full of shame and guilt over their past, and pursued by shadowy figures while lost in the dark night?

Limping to the manger, you witness pure truth wrapped in cloths. The Son of Man came to seek and save those who are weak and full of sorrow. He gave his life as a ransom for many. Jesus later told Pilate he came to testify to the truth.

While visiting the manger and looking at the King come down from his throne for you, dare to embrace the truth; in Christ, you're a new creation—a new babe in him.

Lord, I praise you, the one and only, for revealing your glory. I'm grateful you came to take the heavy load, which I wasn't meant to carry, off my shoulders. Amen.

Luke 2:12, 19:10; Mark 10:45; John 18:37

The First Manger Scene

St. Francis of Assisi had the idea for Christmas Eve, in 1223, to show the people of Greccio the moment Jesus was born. He gathered animals, set up a manger in a cave near town, and invited them to come. As they approached the manger, the townspeople were overcome with emotion, realizing their hearts were as empty as the manger's hay. They dropped to their knees praying and longing for the Christ Child. God opened their eyes of faith for each to see the wiggling, breathing tiny child moving about in the hay.

There's a miracle waiting for you when admitting your heart is empty and asking the Father for eyes of faith to witness the babe's birth, hear the angels rejoicing, and hang out with the shepherds. You're invited to receive God's gift of love—his Son given so that you might live.

As you begin to believe the purpose of the Messiah's coming, the cross stands in the far-off distance. Jesus journey from Bethlehem to Golgotha was his choice, and by his wounds, you are healed.

Lord, I pray for eyes of faith to be a witness to the Messiah's birth. I pray for courage to receive the precious gift of your Son. Amen.

1 PETER 2:24

Born for You to Be Born Again

The world suggests fear is in charge and hope seems so distant. Profits and manipulation are the driving force of corporations, while homeless people live outside their doors. Feeling shame from the past, being weary and burdened in the present, and having no hope for the future all comes from the enemy. He is the great liar and deceiver. He comes hard in an all-out frontal assault to steal your passion for the upcoming celebration of the birth of Christ. Be encouraged; the King left his throne to come and destroy the works of the devil.

Trust Jesus came for you, so you can have an intense excitement for celebrating. This is a challenge, yet Christ offers comfort, stability, and the peace you've been searching for all your life. The Lord himself gives you a sign: the virgin conceived and gave birth to a son. The Father desires to conceive something in you so extraordinary you cannot deny it.

Renew your journey with child-like faith, to witness the light which can never be extinguished. Renew your passion for him; he endured his passion for you. Jesus was born for you, so that you might be born again.

Lord, I pray to believe with more passion that you are the Christ and that I'm born again and will see your kingdom. Amen.

JOHN 10:10; 1 JOHN 3:8, 5:1; ISAIAH 7:14

Jesus Left His Throne for You

The shepherds said to each other, "Come on, let's go to Bethlehem!" They ran to see the baby, lying in the manger. The shepherds told everyone what had happened; and then they went back to their fields and flocks, glorifying and praising God. Eight days later, the baby was named *Jesus*, the name given him by the angel before he was conceived, and as Isaiah wrote 700 years earlier! The witnesses to the coming of the shepherd of the world were shepherds who were watching and guarding their flocks.

You've heard that Jesus is the reason for the season. You're the reason he came, the reason for you to recover, and the reason to hang on one more day. He's the reason to not give up, the light shining in your dark place, until the day dawns and the morning star rises in your heart.

The world's never been the same; you don't need to remain the same. The King of Kings and Lord of Lords left his throne for you. He's the reason to receive him.

Lord, I'm so thankful your light from on high illuminated my dark night when in the shadow of death. You're the reason I'm alive. Amen.

LUKE 1:79, 2:15-21; ISAIAH 7:14; 1 TIMOTHY 6:15; 2 PETER 2:19

Receive the Father's Gift

This Christmas is a celebration of being sober and clean. The memory of past celebrations can induce shame and guilt. You might have *done* it, but Jesus came to declare, you're *not* it! You've been around the block a time or two, yet God used every disaster, failure, and regret to lead you to the manger. As his star reaches down, God's light begins to shine in your heart and give you the light of the knowledge of the glory of God in the face of Christ.

Allow God to gently bring you to his gift. The wonder of Jesus' birth in Bethlehem can be your rebirth as a new person in recovery. Smile with joy as you take his hand; Jesus became human to experience what you've been through.

The shepherds couldn't keep the good news quiet; they had to tell everyone they saw what happened. You can still visit the manger, and share with others what you hear and see.

Lord, I'm totally amazed and humbled you chose to gift your Son to me. I come to your manger to bow down and worship you and kneel before Christ, my Lord. Amen.

2 CORINTHIANS 4:6; JOHN 1:14

The Celebration Need Not End

God's the champion of lost causes. He protected you from self-destruction to be born again. The divine mystery of how God chose to enter this world drives the Pharisees and intellectuals a bit wacky. Jesus could have come as a majestic king on the throne. Only in child-like faith can you wrap your busy mind around this great event—Jesus in the flesh, *Immanuel*. His parents were a woman, pregnant by the Holy Spirit, and a man, shamed because of Mary's pregnancy before marriage.

A group of poor, smelly, dirty, shepherds responded to the angels' message by running to see the babe who brought heaven to earth. Jesus invites you to his come-as-you-are party. Do you run or quicken your pace? Do you drop everything when angels sing? Do you bow and kneel to a baby?

The only thing that separates the men from boys, the women from girls, and the spiritual from religious at Christmas will be their degree of intimate passion for Jesus. In him and through faith in him you may approach the Son of God this Christmas with freedom and confidence.

Lord, I pray to celebrate your birth each day I'm breathing. It's been a great birthday party, and I don't want it to end. I thank you for the light which lights my path. Amen.

EPHESIANS 3:12

Yeshua

As I glanced up at the star,
So close, so near, yet so far,
Knowing from heaven above,
God's child born to love…
A precious one has come.

On journey to manger, an angel's voice,
Cuts through the mind's chaos and noise.
No door, no floor, I see the child,
At peace, so vulnerable, so tiny, so mild…
His heart's light, shines so bright.

He's come to save the lost,
His price for me, a high cost,
A time from his Father apart,
Compassion flows from his radiant heart.

When I hear Yeshua, his holy name,
Nothing, never, ever can be the same.

-MIKE SHEA

It Will Be Alright

Dachau Concentration Camp, where hundreds of thousands were killed because they were Jewish, was located across a road from the city where people worked and lived. There's a story of a father returning after the day's hard labor to discover one of his sons missing. His remaining son told him a soldier had taken him away. He then realized his wife was gone. She had pushed through the soldiers, grabbed her son's hand and said, "My dear son, it will be alright. I am with you!"

That night, in their grief, the son whispered, "Dad, I'm scared!" The father grabbed his hand, "My dear son, it will be alright. I am with you."

The same satanic forces that worked to exterminate God's chosen people during the Holocaust are the same forces out to kill, steal, and destroy God's calling on your life. The Son of God was arrested, condemned, thrown into the Pharisee Concentration Camp, tortured, and brutally murdered for you. Absolutely nothing can separate you from his love—the demons and the powers of hell can't keep God's love away.

God's reaching his hand to you in recovery. Grab on tightly as he whispers, "My dear child, it will be alright. I am with you."

Lord, I pray for compassion to know others are going through times of great tribulation. I'm so grateful you're always with me. Amen.

John 10:10; Romans 8:38

Do You Know?

Do you know the King of Kings and the Lord of Lords is the only one death can't touch?
Do you know you're the beloved of Jesus?
Do you know it's your season to receive what God has already done for you?
Do you know you're worthy to have life spoken over you?
Do you know to seek God first is your most important task?
Do you know God put you before his Son?
Do you know your recovery will glorify God?
Do you know there's no condemnation when in Christ?
Do you know the minimum in recovery is not enough?
Do you know whatever you invest in, that's where your treasure is?
Do you know you are to be a good steward of what God's entrusted you with?
Do you know whatever Jesus promised—it is, and you are a keeper of that promise?
Do you know it's God's plan for you to prosper and flourish?
Do you know Jesus took your shame and guilt and nailed it to the cross?
Do you know the blood of Jesus cleanses you from every sin?
Do you know God forgets you ever sinned?
Do you know your addiction was a blessing, and recovery a gift?

Lord, thanks for the wisdom to know I can activate what you know by just saying yes. I pray for willingness to know more about you. Amen.

Romans 8:1; Jeremiah 29:11, 31:34; Colossians 2:14; 1 John 1:7

Believe the Truth before the Lie

When you trust God, your faith is the confidence that what you hope for will actually happen. These words of truth give comfort to know all is well. God wants to take your worries, frustrations, and fear. Hope is a strong and trustworthy anchor for your soul, and ushers you into God's inner sanctuary. His light breathes life into your hopes and dreams, and gently brings them into reality. Go to the source of hope and get filled, so your overflow of joy and peace can be a gift to others.

The enemy's counterfeits are fear, lack of hope, and depression. Fear is about punishment, but the Father's perfect love drives out fear and kicks it back to hell where it came from. Don't accept a lie from the devil, before receiving God's truth.

The stumbling block is waiting for his perfect timing and guidance to work your recovery according to his plan where his peace flourishes in the midst of life's trials and tests. Trust God's plan is better than yours.

Lord, thanks for your Spirit who guides me into all truth, and tells me about the future I thought was lost. I pray to believe the truth before the lie. Amen.

HEBREWS 11:1, 6:9; ROMANS 15:13; PROVERBS 3:5-6; JOHN 16:13

A Mainline Blessing

It's frustrating when seeking a mainline blessing with a sideline commitment. Get off the bench and let perseverance finish its work that you may not lack anything. God is inviting you to participate in your recovery. Practice the life-changing principles you're learning during your daily walk. It's essential to take the necessary time for devotions. The Word of God is alive and active; it shows you the truth, exposes the flesh, corrects mistakes, and trains you to live God's way.

The King of the universe desires you to place the extraordinary gift of your heart into his loving hands. Serenity is the place where you can do all things through him who gives you strength. By God's grace, you step out of adversity into his peace, regardless of the circumstances that come at you today.

As God nudges you to leave the sidelines and stop being a spectator, his light shines brightly to reveal the path prepared for you. Your mainline blessing is knowing you were once lost in addiction and now have been brought near through the blood of Christ into recovery.

Lord, I pray for grace to get as close to you as I can and rest in your lap. I pray I will be diligent in my devotions to know you more. Amen.

JAMES 1:4-5; HEBREWS 4:12; 2 TIMOTHY 3:16-17; PHILIPPIANS 4:13; EPHESIANS 2:13

Admit You Are Weak

In recovery, you grasp the truth that God spoke the word that healed and rescued you from the grave. In the nick of time, he gently lifted you from the chaos which threatened your very existence, and placed you in recovery.

God invites you to give thanks for his unfailing love, and tell others that his love is available to all. No more playing games, people pleasing, or manipulating. What a tall order! Trust God's Spirit to go through and get to your inner being. It's an inside job; just let go and let God.

Accepting you're powerless, and knowing you can't do it on your own, gets you to take the first step to thank God and praise his name. It's okay not to be okay, to admit weakness, to come to the end of yourself, and to let go. God's grace is sufficient for you. Your weakness is exchanged for Christ's strength, which empowers you to say "no" to the flesh and "not this time" to the lie of the enemy. The weaker you get, the stronger you become.

Lord, I pray your grace is sufficient and the weaker I get, the stronger I become. I'm grateful I don't need to figure this out in my busy mind. Amen.

PSALMS 100:4,107:20-22; 2 CORINTHIANS 12:9

My Thoughts

ABOUT THE AUTHOR

I entered Minnesota Adult and Teen Challenge 11 years ago, and have been part of a faith-based recovery ministry since. These pages contain essential, yet practical, tools for those who are sick of being sick and tired of living underneath what God has for them. It's God's grace and tender mercy that has gifted me the freedom from active addiction to write the *New Day, New Me* devotional journal, and now, *Serenity* the daily devotional, in a span of eight months. My heart's desire is that this daily devotional will be your doorway to discover you can never do anything to get God to love you more, or less. His love is unconditional and he pursues you relentlessly for a relationship. I pray you experience true freedom, one day at a time.

Mike Shea

www.SerenityVillage.net
www.serenityvillagecc.org